DINÉ IDENTITY IN A TWENTY-FIRST-CENTURY WORLD

DINÉ
IDENTITY
IN A 21ST-CENTURY
WORLD

LLOYD L. LEE

THE UNIVERSITY OF
ARIZONA PRESS
TUCSON

The University of Arizona Press
www.uapress.arizona.edu

© 2020 by The Arizona Board of Regents
All rights reserved. Published 2020

ISBN-13: 978-0-8165-4068-6 (paper)

Cover design by Leigh McDonald
Cover art: *Essence* by Venaya Yazzie
Interior by Sara Thaxton
Typeset in Times New Roman (text), Insignia LT Std, and Myriad Pro (display)

Library of Congress Cataloging-in-Publication Data
Names: Lee, Lloyd L., 1971– author.
Title: Diné identity in a twenty-first-century world / Lloyd L. Lee.
Description: Tucson : The University of Arizona Press, 2020. | Includes bibliographical
    references and index.
Identifiers: LCCN 2019046618 | ISBN 9780816540686 (paperback)
Subjects: LCSH: Navajo Indians—Ethnic identity.
Classification: LCC E99.N3 L536 2020 | DDC 305.897/26—dc23
LC record available at https://lccn.loc.gov/2019046618

CONTENTS

ACKNOWLEDGMENTS

This book is one of a four-part series on Diné peoples and the Navajo Nation. The first book explored Diné perspectives on reclaiming and revitalizing Navajo thought. The second book envisioned Navajo Nation sovereignty and called for the rethinking of Navajo sovereignty rooted in Diné ways and values. This is the third book in the series, focusing on Diné identity markers in history, philosophy, language, relations, and the land.

The series is my effort to contribute to the continuance of the Navajo Nation, Diné peoples, and Indigenous communities. My parents, immediate family, other relatives, friends, colleagues, and peoples have influenced and affected my scholarship and underscored the importance of contributing to the Navajo Nation and Indigenous peoples. I want to thank all my family, other relatives, friends, and colleagues.

I want to thank the individuals who participated in my dissertation study on Navajo cultural identity when I was a doctoral candidate. Some of their perspectives are included in this text. Their willingness to share their thoughts and experiences was tremendous and important to a young student trying to understand what Navajo cultural identity is and the influences in life that shape and mold it.

I want to recognize several colleagues at the University of New Mexico. They are amazing and hard working human beings and scholars who do so much for their Native nations, Indigenous communities, and humanity. They inspire me. Thank you, Wendy S. Greyeyes, Tiffany S. Lee, Leola Tsinnajinnie-Paquin, Robin Minthorn, Glenabah Martinez, Gregory A. Cajete, Melanie K. Yazzie, Vincent Werito, and Shawn Secatero.

DINÉ IDENTITY IN A TWENTY-FIRST-CENTURY WORLD

Introduction

On November 11, 2011, the Navajo Office of Vital Records launched new identification (ID) cards at the Navajo Nation Museum in Window Rock, Arizona. The ID cards were the size of a driver's license, with name, birth date, gender, physical characteristics, mailing address, signature, date of issue, and expiration date. They also listed the person's tribal enrollment number. The Office of Vital Records and the Navajo Nation were hoping to make the new ID cards an acceptable replacement for the federal Certificate of Degree of Indian Blood to prove tribal membership.

The initial cost of the card was seventeen dollars, and it was valid for four years. The card could indicate veteran status if the person submitted a Certificate of Release or Discharge from active duty (DD-214 form). The goal was to have each Navajo citizen carrying an ID. The card had several security features, including a holographic Navajo Nation seal and machine-readable zone, which contains the cardholder's personal information in a format U.S. border agents at the Canada and Mexico border can scan. The ID cards were designed to make it difficult to fraudulently reproduce. Then President Ben Shelly and Vice

President Rex Lee Jim received their ID cards at the time. Since 2011, however, only a small number of Diné people have ID cards. Most people continue to use the federal Certificate of Degree of Indian Blood for tribal membership.

Diné identity in the twenty-first century is distinctive and personal. It is a mixture of traditions, customs, values, behaviors, technologies, worldviews, languages, and lifeways. Diné identity is analogous to Diné weaving, in that it interweaves all of life's elements together.

In this book, I investigate Diné/Navajo identity markers. The markers are Diné baa hane' (Navajo history), Są'áh Naagháí Bik'éh Hózhóón (SNBH, a foundational worldview), Diné bizaad (language), k'é (relations), k'éí (clanship), and Níhi Kéyah (Diné land). These markers represent past, present, and future elements of a Diné way of life. Several Diné persons share their perspectives on the different markers, and I include non-Diné scholarship as well. The non-Diné scholarship is a small representation of observed and recorded cultural practices and ways. Diné scholarship is the primary source of information.

When examining the literature on Diné people, culture, history, education, language, health, law, and economics are prevalent topics. In this introduction, I discuss and analyze selected texts researching Diné women and worldview. These texts provide background information on the markers and chapters.

Diné women are an integral part of cultural continuance, family dynamics, and a Diné way of life. When a child is born, the child is of their mother's clan. The child(ren) is a mother's possession. Diné women have direct power and authority to determine the leadership in the extended family networks and community systems.

Diné women are a reflection of Changing Woman, the mother of the Diné people. After a girl has her first period, she goes through a rite of passage, Kinaaldá. The girl has all the power of Changing Woman during the ceremony, and she carries Changing Woman's teachings and values. During this time, a woman is the embodiment of Changing Woman and the values exemplified by her.

Charlotte Frisbie's *Kinaaldá* is a comprehensive description of the girl's puberty ceremony.[1] Navajo women and men are both supposed to go through a puberty ceremony. The men's ceremony continues today, but fewer boys participate. Although the boy's ceremony is in resurgence, the number of boys participating is fewer than the number of girls who participate in the Kinaaldá.

In the girl's ceremony, she is instructed on how to live exemplifying Changing Woman and an "ideal" human being. The ceremony and instructions are in the Diné language. From this point forward, the girls are no longer treated as girls; they are women and must behave and be respected in the appropriate manner. Frisbie describes the stories and texts of some of the songs of the ceremony. Her description provides the reader with a glimpse into a sacred experience for Diné people.

Kinaaldá describes a meaningful and beautiful picture of a Diné ceremony. A woman's physical, emotional, spiritual, and mental health is sacred and essential to a Diné way of life. Diné people appreciate the Kinaaldá. They want these ceremonial ways to continue.

Ruth Roessel's *Women in Navajo Society* explores the role of a traditional Diné woman. In the introduction, she provides advice, guidance, and help to Diné women and the people. Roessel explains what a Diné woman needs to do in child rearing, marriage, puberty rites, and leadership, as well as what needs to be accomplished in the seasons. She reflects on school, home, and her upbringing. Her personal reflections show her growth as a Diné woman.

In those days, because we had very little money we were not able to buy much food at the trading post. Yet, my family would try to take care of other people who came and needed help. I remember my parents giving them watermelons, corn, squashes, pumpkins, and so forth. The good that we grew was food that we were able to eat and that we did not have to pay for. Today we do not have the same kinds of physical hardship that I endured as I grew up. I look back on my childhood with great pride because those were days when I learned responsibility and how to be a Navajo woman.[2]

Roessel worked hard when she was young and learned the values and responsibilities of a Diné woman. The values she learned are elements of her philosophy. The philosophy is tied to cultural knowledge. She states:

> Everything I do grows out of that belief and pride in being a Navajo woman. What I do, what I say and what I am all are parts of being a Navajo. I am proud to be a Navajo woman. I was brought into this world a Navajo girl and I am glad. I believe a person comes into this world to serve others—not herself or himself. As I look at medicine men and women I see people who always help others, always give of themselves, persons who do not try to accumulate material and temporal power—who only want to serve, who only want to be a channel for the Holy People. As I look at Changing Woman and her two sons I see their emphasis on service. So I want to help and serve my people. I want my children to help and serve others. I want other Navajos to grow up and be taught that the higher values are service—not self![3]

Roessel lived to serve and teach others. Her service to Diné people is her identity.

Women in Navajo Society presents cultural knowledge from a Diné woman's perspective; however, the narrative can be interpreted as judgmental. Roessel's text tells people who is Diné and who is not. Yet despite the judgmental tone, the narrative is a key contribution to an understanding of Diné identity.

Charlotte Goodluck's "Understanding Navajo Ethnic Identity: Weaving the Meaning through the Voices of Young Girls" studies the meaning of identity among Diné girls between the ages of nine and fifteen.[4] Goodluck used a qualitative phenomenological methodology to examine how twenty Diné girls defined their identity, including interviews, a participant observation approach, and questionnaire.

Goodluck determines that the Diné girls' identity revolves around "four worlds": (1) personal identity (appearance, living with differences, feeling unique); (2) ethnic identity (ethnic ambiguity, stereotypes, racist experiences, confusion, duality); (3) tribal identity (family, language, religion); and (4) moving between worlds (geographic location, changes, visits to grandmother). She further describes these worlds using metaphors, such as weaving, pottery, dance, and corn pollen journey. The metaphors' meanings reflect Diné way of life and ethnicity.

Goodluck develops a circular model to reflect the four worlds, which demonstrates Diné female identity as multidimensional, dynamic, and constantly changing. She uses social work theories, like orthogonal cultural identification theory, in her analysis and determines it is not a good match for her study. The model she then creates provides a better understanding of the girls' experiences. Although a model is difficult to use across all Diné communities, Goodluck's framework avoids stage development and sequential processes. She recognizes that individuals are human beings.

A model to frame Diné identity in the twenty-first century is challenging. One that allows for complexity and constant change can supply a comprehensive view; however, not every Diné individual fits into such a model. A research project examining such models is warranted.

Amy J. Schulz's article "Navajo Women and the Politics of Identity" focuses on intergenerational changes in the (re)construction of Navajo female identity in social, political, economic, and cultural contexts.[5] Her examination of collective identities and the meanings behind them focus on Indian as a supratribal identity and Navajo as a tribal identity.

She interviewed thirty-one women in three cohorts. The first cohort consisted of Diné women born prior to 1946; the second comprised women born between 1946 and 1960; and the third group included women born between 1961 and 1976. The women she interviewed experienced extended kinship networks, spiritual practices, and the Diné language more than Diné women who lived in urban areas.

Schulz's analysis on the construction of being Indian shows differences in the age cohorts. Interaction with Western society affected how the women defined their Indian identity. The second cohort experienced federal government pressure to not speak the Diné language, the dismantling of Indian rights, decreased livestock and agriculture economies, and increased wage labor work. The youngest cohort group mostly spoke the English language and knew very little Diné. They also grew up in an era when the federal government recognized individual political rights. All three cohorts had similar experiences with the differences between groups of people and unjust generalization. The women espoused that Indians are different from one another, including individuals within the same community.

The women in the cohorts did not want to be given an Indian identity by non-Natives; rather, they saw themselves as Diné. According to Schulz, power relations between Indians and whites were disrupted because of this, and the women constructed their own identities, on their own terms. Schulz identifies the themes of strength, resilience, and survival as the elements of Diné and Indian identity. Nonetheless, each cohort had differences, measured in personal identity.

While many texts examine Navajo women, numerous others also document Diné worldview and philosophy. I analyze the following selected texts in this book.

Miranda Haskie's dissertation "Preserving a Culture: Practicing the Navajo Principles of Hózhó dóó K'é" focuses on the life of her grandfather Albert "Chic" Sandoval Sr. Haskie develops a grounded theory on how individuals from diverse cultural backgrounds can "preserve" their culture in Western society. She generates her theory from investigating her grandfather's life and the Diné principles of family, hózhǫ, and SNBH. She writes, "In order to survive the integration with a dominant culture, the secondary culture must meet certain conditions. When these conditions are met, people successfully preserve their culture. These

conditions include practicing hózhǫ doo k'é, becoming educated, utilizing tools (products of preservation, such as customs that have been
recorded on tape and in books), practicing leadership, changing, and
adapting."[6]
Her research shows how her grandfather was able to maintain and
sustain his Diné identity in juxtaposition with living in Western society.
The study does not, however, thoroughly discuss Sandoval's challenges
and failures, which can provide a holistic perspective on an individual's
identity.

Haskie's dissertation illustrates how a Diné man sustained his identity. Of concern, however, is that the work can be used as a recipe for
Diné identity in the twenty-first century and beyond. Telling people how
to be Diné can be overbearing and intrusive. Western ways, Christianity,
and other worldviews have influenced the Navajo Nation, but these
influences do not necessarily disrupt or eliminate Diné identity. In many
respects, the influences add to twenty-first century Diné identity. Some
may disagree with this assessment. They may say those influences completely change Diné identity. The next text examines this phenomenon
in the mid-twentieth century.

Clyde Kluckhohn's article "The Philosophy of Navaho Indians"
analyzes Diné thought. Kluckhohn studied Diné people and wrote several articles on Diné life, philosophy, and culture.[7] "The Philosophy
of Navaho Indians" describes a philosophical understanding of Diné
culture and life through generalizations of ethical principles, values,
and actions.

He created a chart to gain a better understanding of how a Diné person thought and acted at the time the article was written, in the 1950s.
The chart describes the universe as orderly, with personality, and full
of dangers, where evil and good are complementary, experience is con-
tinuous and primary, and morality is situational, with human relations
premised on family individualism.

Kluckhohn's chart is rather simplistic. Although he gathered information from healers and chanters who are knowledgeable, the knowledge

shared between healer and chanters and the general public is limited because ceremonial and sacred knowledge is not shared with just anyone for any purpose. A person must go through life stages to gain access to Navajo sacred and ceremonial knowledge. Usually the individual is an apprentice of a healer and chanter, so the knowledge Kluckhohn discusses and analyzes is only the beginning. A deeper and more detailed amount of knowledge is not shared without going through the process of becoming a healer and chanter.

Also in the article, Kluckhohn focuses on the impact of white American ideology and ways on Diné premises, values, and ethics. He describes how individuals were moving away from Diné values and ethics: "The introduction of the white idea of individualism without the checks and balances that accompany it leads to the failure of collective or cooperative action of every sort."[8] His interpretations of the changing Diné premises, values, and ethics is limited since he only observed and interacted in one community and not with the entire Navajo Nation. Nonetheless, his article illustrates the effects of Western thought and ways on Diné identity in the mid-twentieth century.

John Farella's *The Main Stalk: A Synthesis of Navajo Philosophy* came out in 1984.[9] In the book, Farella describes an understanding of Navajo philosophy for a non-Navajo audience. He explores Navajo religion and scrutinizes SNBH. He describes Diné thought as connected and interrelated, and he advocates that the Navajo way of life is paradoxical, nondualistic, and realistic in relations to life's wholeness.

Farella explains that the Diyin Dine'é (Holy People) are creative, with excellent sensory skills and the ability to move effortlessly. While his description of these abilities is fine, the key is the significance of the Holy People. They created the Diné people and the world in which we live. The Diné people acknowledge this and respect their teachings.

The primary focus of Farella's study is his discussion of SNBH. He evaluates earlier interpretations by other scholars and focuses on the roots of each word of SNBH. He does not go much into the holistic experience of each human being. The definitions are similar for every

Diné person; however, the experiencing and meaning of SNBH will be different for each individual. The meanings are actually learned and understood as one goes through life.

Wilson Aronilth Jr.'s *Foundation of Culture* contrasts with Kluckhohn and Farella.[10] The book emphasizes Diné values, including clans as a social system, duality, origin, and cultural knowledge. Aronilth shares stories and knowledge on the Diné calendar, language, way of learning, and the clan system. The book is configured in such a way as to allow Diné children to learn core values and apply them in the present day. The content is an introduction and meant to be supplemented with guidance from parents, relatives, and anyone else with Diné cultural knowledge. Aronilth recognizes that what he has written comes from teachers, families, relatives, and life experiences. He does not try to provide a comprehensive description; instead he explains how life experience and community is a grounding of Diné philosophy.

A similar text to Aronilth's is a booklet put together by the Office of Diné Culture and Language in 1992. The title of the booklet is "Diné Traditional Ways, Beliefs, and Values." The content includes a Diné prayer, a meaning in being Diné, a Diné calendar, corn, Diné cradleboard, Diné basket, clan's gish, girl and boy teachings, and the universal elements of water, air, and fire. The booklet, written in English, is an engaging approach to sharing Diné cultural knowledge. While *Foundation of Culture* has similar content to "Diné Traditional Ways, Beliefs, and Values," it does not come across as a recipe for Diné way of life and identity. This booklet does in some respects. The concern is again dictating to Diné individuals the meaning of Diné identity and what a person must do to ensure this recognition. This dictation is a part of Diné essentialism.

In *The Sound of Navajo Country: Music, Language, and Diné Belonging*, Kristina Jacobsen examines how Navajo citizens negotiate points of friction regarding authenticity through sound, speech, and music and how these points of friction affect individual Diné's sense of belonging.[11] The question of authenticity is pertinent and reflects ongoing negotiation and friction for Diné and all Native peoples. For example, in 2014 one of the two finalists for the Navajo Nation presidential general election did not speak Diné bizaad proficiently. Two other candidates who did not make the general election filed grievances against the finalist, which eventually resulted in his disqualification. The third-place finisher in the primary election was promoted to the general election and won the Navajo Nation presidency.

In her study, Jacobsen examines authenticity through blood quantum, heritage-language abilities, place of residence, and taste. Various labels created and used by Diné people reflect these notions of authenticity, such as full blood, full Navajo, traditional, deep rez, real rez, Diné, "john," urban Navajo, and New Mexico Navajo. These labels and the notion of authenticity show the complexity of Diné identity in the twenty-first century. Various distinct labels become attached to individual Diné depending on speech, blood quantum, place of residence, and taste. These distinctions can play in essential ways, leading to divisions in Diné families, communities, and the entire Navajo Nation.

While numerous studies have focused on Diné women and philosophy, my text *Diné Masculinities: Conceptualizations and Reflections* is one of the few on Diné masculinities.[12] *Diné Masculinities* shares thirty Navajo male perspectives in the area of development, performance, and the impact of colonialism. In the examination, Western and Navajo values influence how Navajo men are brought up and develop their manhood. For many of the men in the study, what a man does is his basis of manhood, although some similarity is tied to Western ideology and thought. All the men agree that colonialism has affected their manhood and Navajo men in general; however, the degree of impact is a major difference among the thirty men. Overall, Diné manhood has been influenced by American and Western ideology, values, and thoughts, yet Diné thoughts and ways continue.

These texts provide a lens into Diné identity. Haskie writes about her grandfather's way of preserving Diné culture. Chic Sandoval spoke Diné and English and respected people who spoke both languages. His parents and grandparents taught him the values and ethics to follow based on Diné teachings. He lived an agrarian way of life, herding sheep and growing crops—not many people live this type of lifestyle in the twenty-first century. He spoke Diné, lived on the reservation, and believed in a Diné worldview.

Over three hundred thousand Diné people grew up in different social and physical environments. The differences shape Diné identity and way of life, showing the diversity and vitality of the Diné people. Whether the person chooses to write poetry, tell stories, go to college, become a lawyer, help people speak the Diné language, herd sheep, grow crops, or know very little of Diné cultural knowledge, the person is Diné. Each person represents who the Diné are and who they are becoming. Some may disagree and say Diné identity is changing into something completely different, but this book will show this is not the case.

Frisbie and Roessel reveal that Diné women are strong and resilient. By showing that Diné women have not forgotten who they are as Diné women, Diné identity is sustainable. Kluckhohn points to the influence of white American ideology on Diné premises, ethics, and values. The degree of influence varies with each person and community. Many Diné individuals maintain and sustain Diné identity through speaking the language, participating in ceremonies and traditions, following an SNBH path, believing in core values and ethics, and interweaving a Diné way of life with a present-day lifestyle. The texts explain how Diné individuals negotiate their identity in the twentieth and twenty-first century.

Diné identity is defined in numerous ways in the present. Each definition is acceptable because of the people's diversity. The various definitions are the foundation of the Diné people.

Native nations and communities enroll their citizens via blood quantum and/or lineal descent. In the past, Native nations and communities did not have race-based enrollment; instead, family relations was the standard. In the United States, however, racial identity is a primary method of determining who belongs where and with whom.[13] American colonies set up a series of laws to deny civil rights to African slaves and Native peoples in the early eighteenth century. The colonies wanted to distinguish themselves from people of color, leading to racial stratification.

In the twenty-first century, many Native nations and communities determine their enrollment criteria. The United States Supreme Court affirmed this political power in *Santa Clara Pueblo v. Martinez* (1978). They ruled that Santa Clara Pueblo has the political right to set enrollment standards. At the time of the decision, blood quantum determined enrollment for many Native nations. This enrollment standard primarily remains unchanged.

The Navajo Nation has an official enrollment total of more than three hundred thousand.[14] Individuals who want to enroll in the Navajo Nation must possess one-quarter or more Diné/Navajo blood and be a descendant of a person on the 1940 census roll.

In the 2010 U.S. Census, 332,129 people self-identified themselves as Diné, of which 286,731 identified as only Diné and no other racial group.[15] This strong racial connection is explained in history. Navajo communities maintained a strong connection to the land and a Diné way of life. Diné people for hundreds of years had a physical, social, spiritual, and psychological separation from Western peoples. Yet, interactions between Diné people and other Native peoples did take place.[16] Intertribal relations and marriages occurred with Zuni, Hopi, Apache, Ute, Jemez, and several other Native peoples. These intertribal relations and intermarriages help create new Diné clans and influenced Diné identity. These influences continue to the present, such as practicing Christianity, speaking and writing English, and watching television.

Throughout Navajo history, numerous adaptations are evident, such as with livestock. Sheep, cows, cattle, and horses are a part of a Diné family and way of life. The expansion of Diné weaving is a second example. The incorporation of unique and traditional design elements enhanced the aesthetic value of each Navajo rug and blanket. A third example is the Native American Church. Prior to the twentieth century, Diné people followed a traditional spiritual way. Christianity and the

Native American Church were introduced to the people in the nineteenth and twentieth centuries.

Many Diné view themselves as "full blood" because of past family relatives marrying other Diné. Many assume their ancestors married only Diné people and that intertribal and interracial marriages did not occur. In reality, many Diné people have mixed backgrounds. In the clan system, the four main clans increased to more than sixty.[17] Several clans were created with other Native peoples, such as Naasht'ézhi Dine'é (Zuni clan), Ma'iideeshgiizhnii (Jemez clan), Naakaii Dine'é (Mexican clan), Nooda'i Dine'é (Ute clan), and Naashgali Dine'é (Mescalero Apache clan). The clan system is known as k'éí.

The history of Navajo enrollment is tied to natural resources and constitutional adoption.[18] In 1923, the Navajo government was established without a constitution. In 1937, a general assembly was called to develop a constitution, but it was not adopted. At the time, the primary concern was oversight by the superintendent of Indian affairs. Yet, the 1937 constitution did include a section on membership requirements. The main requirement for Navajo enrollment was to meet the one-quarter blood quantum level.

A second attempt to adopt a constitution occurred in 1953. It also failed, but the section on membership requirements was put into a separate Navajo council resolution and adopted.[19] The requirement stated:

The membership of the Navajo Nation shall consist of the following persons:

(a) All persons of Navajo blood whose name appears on the official roll of the Navajo Tribe maintained by the Bureau of Indian Affairs, as of the date of adoption of this constitution, provided, however, that corrections may be made in said roll for a period of ten years hereafter.

(b) Any person who is at least one-fourth (1/4) degree Navajo blood, but who has not been previously enrolled as a member of the Tribe, is eligible for membership and enrollment.

(c) Children born to any enrolled member of the Navajo Tribe subsequent to the adoption of this constitution shall automatically
become members of the Navajo Tribe, provided they are at least of
one-fourth degree Navajo blood.[20]

The resolution was designed to be temporary but became permanent
and now is codified as Navajo Nation law. No amendments have been
made to this law since the adoption in 1953. In spring 2004, legislation
was introduced in the Navajo Nation Council by then council delegate
Ervin Keeswood from Hogback chapter to lower the blood quantum
requirement to one-eighth. The resolution failed.[21]

This book does not examine authenticity and essentialism; rather, it
considers Diné identity markers. These markers show how Diné people's identity is a combination of past and present ways and thought. All
Diné peoples reflect the tapestry of Diné identity. For instance, some
Diné speak the language fluently, while others do not; some know or
sing the ceremonial songs, while others do not; some pray in Diné,
while others do not; and some know their clans' histories, while others
do not. These differences continue.

The goal for this book is to describe Diné identity in terms of the
people's history, way of life, thought, language, and distinctiveness.
This book is in no way intended to declare the "true and authentic" Diné
person. While this book cannot answer all the questions surrounding
Diné identity, it will consider the following queries:

1. What are Diné identity markers?
2. What is the history of Diné identity?

This book contributes to specific Native Nation–centered scholarship. Diné histories are vital to the people but also to the broader scope
of Native American and American history. An understanding of Diné
identity is meaningful to comprehending how individuals live and how
their way of life matures. Since creation, Diné people have adapted to

Figure 1 Navajo baskets made out of yarn by the author's aunt.

their physical and social environment; however, American colonialism has influenced Diné identity. This influence plays a significant role in how Diné people frame their identity.

The Diné people call themselves Diné (People), Nihokáá Dine'é (Earth Surface People), Bíla'ashla'ii Dine'é (Five-Fingered Human Beings), and the Diyin Nohookáá Dine'é (Holy Earth Surface People).

All these terminologies refer to the Diné people. What follows is a look into specific Diné identity markers bringing relevancy to these terminologies.

The book is for a diverse audience, not solely academic. It is a text on Diné identity rather than an academic enterprise with theoretical advances. The discussion on identity is personal and from a Diné-centric worldview. This worldview is reflective and conversational rather than purely critical. An analytical lens is included, but the book's foundation is from a Diné perspective.

The book is organized as follows: chapter 1 describes Diné baa hane' (Navajo history), focusing on events illustrating the strength of the people; chapter 2 discusses SNBH (foundational worldview); chapter 3 examines Diné bizaad (language); chapter 4 reviews k'é (relations) and k'éí (clanship); chapter 5 takes up Níhi Kéyah (Diné land) and shares individual perspectives on what the land means to each person; and the conclusion considers the future implications for Diné identity. Repeated information is shared in several of the markers. The repetition reflects the interweaving of these elements and not distinct silos.

ONE

Diné Baa Hane'

N
avajo history provides a foundational understanding of Diné identity. What events affected the people? How did the Diné people come to be?

Every human group has a starting point, an origin, an emergence to this planet and universe. The Navajo emergence story is core to the people. The story described in this chapter is one perspective. Some Diné healers, storytellers, and families may have different versions. I do not want to espouse one narrative as correct and the others wrong. The various narratives are valid because each comes from the people. The version used in this chapter is from *Navajo History*, volume 1, published by the Navajo Curriculum Center at Rough Rock Community School and edited by Ethelou Yazzie in 1971.[1] The narrative is a Navajo storytelling perspective, a telling of experiences, not a chronological account. It is Navajo history, not a film or a timeline. Experiences are the foundation of the narratives and do not focus on the year. For the next several pages, the reader needs to understand that these narratives represent the identity of the people, the land, and the universes. It is not to be judged in a way intended to dispute the narratives.

In the First World, entities lived with one another, although no human beings existed.[2] The world was black and contained within four corners. The east cloud corner column is called folding dawn; the south corner column is folding sky blue; the west corner column is folding twilight; and the north corner column is folding darkness.

The First World was small and similar to living in a sea of water mist. First Man (Áłtsé Hastiin) and white corn (doo honoot'ínii) were formed in the east by the combination of white and black clouds. One group living in the First World was the wóláchíí dine'é (insect beings). They had constructed a way of life where approval for developing projects and plans required everyone's participation. A model for a consensus government was established. Other beings in the First World included spider ants (na'ashjé'íí), wasp people (tsís'náłtsooí), black ants (wóláchíí), beetles (níłtsągo'), dragonflies (tániil'áí), bat people (jaa'abaní), Spider Man (Na'ashjé'íí Hastiin), and Spider Woman (Na'ashjé'ii Asdzą́ą́). Each of these entities had powers.

On the west side of the First World, First Woman (Áłtsé Asdzą́ą́) and yellow corn originated with the combination of yellow and blue clouds. Along with yellow and white corn, other elements developed: white shell and turquoise for First Woman, and crystal and black jet for First Man.

First Man and First Woman each made fires by burning crystal and turquoise respectively. They saw each other's fire and searched for one another. They met up, and after some time, they came to live with one another.

After a while, various entities disagreed and fought with each other. Living space also became smaller. To ease these problems, they decided to go to another world. They found an opening in the east and entered the Second World, the blue world.

Other entities living in the blue world were blue birds (dólii), blue hawks (ginítsoh dootł'izh), blue jays (joo'gii), blue herons (táłtł'ááh ha'alééh), and other blue-feathered beings. First Man took with him four pillars of light. He, along with Tobacco Hornworm, lighted them.

The Second World contained several different chambers. Other entities lived in these chambers, including wolves (mą'iitsoh), wildcats (náshdóí), badgers (nahashch'id), kit foxes (mą'ii bijaa'tsohí), and mountain lions (náshdóítsoh). The wolves lived in white houses in the east; wildcats lived in blue houses in the south; kit foxes lived in yellow houses in the west; and mountain lions lived in black houses in the north. Each entity was at war with one another. First Man killed some of these entities, although he brought them back to life because they presented him with certain powers, songs, and prayers.

Coyote searched the Second World and found suffering. All entities from the First World wanted to leave. First Man agreed to leave, but before they left, he took away all their bad power. To initiate leaving the Second World, First Man set up a streak of zigzag lightning in the east, along with a streak of straight lightning to the south, a rainbow to the west, and a sunray to the north. The attempt failed. He rotated all four objects in each direction, but all attempts failed. After pondering how to fix the problem, First Man constructed a wand (k'eet'áán) made out of the four sacred minerals brought from the First World. Four footprints were placed on the wand so the entities could stand on the footprints to be carried to the Third World. Before they could stand on the wand and footprints, they had to make a sacrifice (bi yeel). What type of sacrifice the entities made is uncertain. Nonetheless, the people climbed up into the Third World through an opening in the south.

Blue bird was the first to reach the Third World, and others soon followed. Two rivers, one flowing north to south and the other east to west, crossed each other, and the place where the two rivers crossed one another is called Tó Ałnáozlí (crossing of waters). Another name for this place is Tó Bił Dahisk'id (place where the waters crossed). These two rivers, along with six mountains, became the cornerstone for Níhi Kéyah (Diné land) in the Fifth World. The six mountains are Sis Naajiní (White Shell Mountain), Tsoodził (Turquoise Mountain), Dook'o'oosłííd (Abalone Shell Mountain), Dibé Nitsaa (Obsidian

Mountain), Dził Ná'oodiłii (Banded Rock Mountain), and Ch'óol'į́'į́ (Gobernador Knob).

In the Third World, Dootł'iizhiii Ashkii (Turquoise Boy) lived in the east, and Yoołgai Asdzą́ą́ (White Shell Woman) lived in the west. Several other entities called the Third World home, such as dłoziłgai (squirrels), hazéíts'ósii (chipmunks), na'at's'ǫǫsí (mice), tązhii (turkeys), mą'iiłtsóí (foxes), bįįh (deer), mósí (cats), na'ashjé'ii (spider people), na'ashǫ́'iłbáhí (lizards), and na'ashǫ́'ii (snakes). In the Third World, coyote created a serious situation. Coyote pleaded with First Man to give him white shell. First Man did. Coyote took the piece of white shell to the water's edge. He dropped the piece of white shell into a whirlpool and caused it to move up and down four times. On the last cycle, coyote noticed the child of Tééhoołtsódii (Water Monster). Coyote grabbed the baby. Soon after, rain began to fall, causing a flood. First Man requested everyone to meet at Sis Naajiní. First Man gathered pieces from all six mountains. At Sis Naajiní, First Man attempted to grow a tree. The first three attempts failed. On the fourth try, however, a female reed grew to the top of the world. All entities climbed up, but the flood followed.

The entities entered the Fourth World, where they noticed coyote was hiding something under his coat. They searched him and found a baby, Tééhoołtsódii biyázhí (Water Monster's baby). The entities reasoned that the flood occurred because coyote had taken the baby, so they instructed coyote to return the baby to Tééhoołtsódii. A white shell basket of nitł'iz (precious stones) was also offered. Water Monster accepted the baby and the gift, whereupon the flood subsided. The Fourth World was barren and small, so they decided to leave. They climbed up into an opening in the sky to the Fifth World, the glittering world.

Wíineeshch'įįdii (locust) was the first to enter the Fifth World. Water was everywhere. Locust encountered black water bird, who told locust to leave unless locust could pass tests. The first test was to sit in one place for four days. Locust agreed, leaving his shell skin in one place to make it look as if he were sitting in the same place. He passed the first test. A second test asked the locust to draw an arrow through his body. Locust passed the second test. Black water bird believed locust possessed great medicine and swam away to the east. Blue, yellow, and white water birds tested locust, and locust passed all. When all the water birds left, locust was sitting on land, the earth. Mud covered the Fifth World, but the winds dried the land. The rest of the entities followed up into the Fifth World. They emerged through a lake surrounded by four mountains, at a place called Hajíínéí.

The world of the Diné people came into shape from this time onward, including the construction of the first hogan, the taking of the first sweat bath, the establishment of the four seasons, the creation of day and night, the placement of the stars in the sky, and the coming existence of the sun and moon.[3] Morals and ethics are learned after each experience. Listeners to the emergence narratives hear the consequences of improper behavior and learn about the difficulties that may ensue through carelessness or thoughtlessness.[4]

An important entity in Navajo history is born in the Fifth World, 'Asdzą́ą́ Nádleehé (Changing Woman). She was born on the top of Ch'óol'į́'į́ (Gobernador Knob) and became a full-grown woman in twelve days. To recognize her transition to womanhood, a ceremony was organized and conducted. Several entities conducted the first Kinaaldá (Walk in Beauty ceremony) for her. Haashch'éé̗łti'í (Talking God) performed the final night ceremony. Talking God sang twelve hogan songs (hooghan biyiin) still sung today.

Changing Woman gave birth to twin boys who became known as Tó Bájísh Chíní (Child Born of Water) and Naayéé' Neezghání (Monster Slayer). The brothers embarked on long and challenging journeys to visit their father, the Sun. The Sun gave them weapons to fight the monsters plaguing the people at the time. The twins killed Yé'iitsoh T'áá̗łá'í Naagháii (One Walking Giant). Yé'iitsoh's dried blood can be seen in the form of the lava escarpment and beds near Tsoodził (current Mount Taylor). The twins also killed Tsé Nináhálééh (Monster Bird) living on top of Tsé Bit'a'í (Shiprock).

The entities suffered through hardships and challenges early on in the Fifth World. Livestock helped the entities survive the hardship and challenges. One narrative attributes Changing Woman with creating livestock, while another narrative tells of the Sun providing livestock to his twin sons to take back to the people.

Changing Woman created the first four Diné clans. She rubbed her skin from four different areas of her body—her breast, back, and under each arm—to create Kinyaa'áanii, Honágháahnii, Tódích'íi'nii, and Hashtł'ishnii clans.[5]

Critical elements such as hózhǫ́, hózhǫ́ǫ́jí, and cultural knowledge came from this time. As each Navajo generation continues, narratives are passed down so the linkage to the past/emergence remains intact.

Diné people came into contact with human beings and entities. Interactions with the Pueblos, Hopis, Utes, Comanches, and several Native communities influenced Diné identity.

Interactions with Pueblos, Hopis, Utes, Comanches, and Native Peoples

Diné people lived in an area known as Dinétah, east of present-day Farmington, New Mexico. Archaeologists and anthropologists estimate that Diné people entered the region between the twelfth and fifteenth centuries. Diné narratives tell of an even longer period of living in the region. Klara Kelley and Harris Francis's *A Diné History of Navajoland* shows a much longer connection to the region.

Diné people traded and expanded around Dinétah after the emergence to the Fifth World. The entities brought animals and knowledge from four previous worlds. The people faced many challenges during this time. Diné worldview did not differ in the Fifth World from the previous four. The way of life expanded with the knowledge gained with each experience.

After Changing Woman created the four main clans, the people of the four clans spread out to different locations. They encountered Native peoples such as the Hopis, Utes, Apaches, and Comanches. They established extensive trading networks. Relations developed, leading to population increase and new clans.

The people created two types of house dwellings, a female and a male hogan.[6] The female is a cribbed-log house, while the male is forked-pole shaped. The male hogan is made of three forked poles, with the bases set in the ground at the north, south, and west direction of a circle and the forked ends interlocked at the top to brace them in place. Two poles standing up against the interlocked forks from the east, or the "first light of dawn," form the entryway. After the poles are in place to fill the openings between the main forks and the entry, the structure is covered with earth, except for the entry and smoke hole.[7] A vestibule is sometimes added to the structure. A blanket covers the doorway. Diné people adapted to the environment to build better and stronger homes. They observed what physical materials were conducive to life and modified them in distinctly Diné ways.

The migration from Dinétah to other locations continued. A Western centralized government did not exist among the people between AD 700 and 1400.[8] Diné people were organized into autonomous groups with localized leadership; no unified "Western nation-state" with a single leader existed. The clan heads served as the leaders of these autonomous groups, which were the basis of a person's identity. Intertribal relations were a part of the communities' foundation. The people continued to add new experiences to their identities.

European Invasion and Settlement

The first Europeans to invade Níhi Kéyah were the Spanish conquistadors. The Spanish conquistadors and later Mexican peoples affected Native peoples' architecture, agriculture, and social relations. The Spanish conquistadors brought livestock: horses, sheep, goats, cattle, and pigs. Although this is a topic of some debate, many Diné believe Changing Woman introduced livestock. Changing Woman is viewed as a deity. Deities work in mysterious ways, and the introduction of livestock by the Spanish conquistadors can be viewed as Changing Woman helping the people. The debate of the livestock origin is secondary to the overall importance of what occurred after the introduction of the sheep.

Sheep influenced Diné people significantly. The peoples' skills as farmers and their ability to care for their sheep provided the base for social cooperation and mutual interdependence.[9] The sheep became the basis of livelihood. Many Diné people acquired sheep through the growth of a new sheep crop, trading with other Native communities, primarily the Pueblos, and through excursions. The sheep population boomed in the eighteenth and nineteenth centuries. The people became a powerful Native nation through the acquisition of sheep herds; population and territory expanded.

Spanish and Navajo interaction was sporadic and isolated because the conquistadors were more concerned with the Pueblos along the Rio Grande River. The Spanish also did not have a clear understanding of which Native groups they were dealing with from one moment to the next. They eventually recognized the many autonomous Diné clan groups because of a shared common language, rituals, values, and traditions. The Spanish had a slave system in the seventeenth and eighteenth centuries. Hundreds of Diné women and children were enslaved to Spanish viceroys, landowners, and influential people of the Spanish Empire.[10]

From the 1600s to the 1800s, various conflicts arose between the Spanish and Diné people. One such conflict occurred in 1805 at Canyon de Chelly, located in the northeastern part of the current state of Arizona. Diné people know the conflict as Massacre Cave.[11] The Spanish, led by a Sonoran man named Antonio Narbona, killed more than one hundred Diné women, children, and elders. Narbona had hundreds of men from Sonora and more than one hundred New Mexicans on the campaign into parts of Níhi Kéyah. Diné conflicts with the Utes, Comanches, and Pueblos continued as well. The Spanish and later Mexicans allied against the Diné people.

Not all Diné were unified in their efforts against non-Diné; one group under duress allied themselves with the Spanish and later with the Mexicans.[12] This group is known as Diné Anaa'i (Enemy Navajos). Their continued alliances with the Spanish, Mexicans, and later with Americans separated them from the larger group of Diné.[13]

Conflicts continued in the early part of the nineteenth century with the Spanish, Mexicans, and neighboring Native communities. Two examples are the Mexican expedition to Navajo country in 1835 and the Diné attack on the Hopi village of Oraibi in 1837. The Mexican expedition in 1835 resulted in the defeat of an alliance army between the Mexicans and several allies from Jemez Pueblo by more than two hundred Diné men led by an elder man named Narbona, not related to the Sonoran Antonio Narbona. In the second conflict, several hundred Diné men attacked Oraibi to seek revenge for a young Diné man's death at the hands of a Hopi. Many Hopis were killed.[14]

Even with continued conflicts, Diné people were influenced by intertribal marriages and cultural adaptations. Raising livestock and growing corn and other crops became the primary basis of the Diné economy. The evolution of weaving and silversmithing came into form in the 1700s and 1800s. Both became fundamental elements of Diné identity.

American Invasion and Settlement

Life for the people changed with the defeat of the Mexicans by the Americans in the U.S.-Mexico War in 1848. The U.S. government had to protect "peaceable inhabitants" from all Native peoples in the newly "acquired" lands.[15] Military conflicts with Americans increased in the late 1840s through the early 1860s. Fort Defiance was built during this period, in 1851. The United States claimed that Diné people posed an imminent danger and an obstacle to economic prosperity.

From 1846 to 1868, seven different treaties were signed between the Diné people and the U.S. government. The U.S. Senate ratified only two of the seven treaties. These treaties were designed to subdue the people and decrease Diné authority in the Southwest. Americans viewed Navajos as inhuman and savage-like, and strongly believed they needed to be killed or civilized. Many non-Natives did not believe "civilization" was possible, as one Santa Fe resident huffed, "You might as well make a hyena adopt the habits of a poodle dog."[16]

U.S. General James H. Carleton, in charge of New Mexico Territory in 1862, implemented a plan to deal with the "Navajo problem," which called for all Diné to be placed on a single reservation, Fort Sumner, in a remote area in what is now southeastern New Mexico.[17] Segregation and assimilation were imposed on the Diné people at Fort Sumner.[18] More than ten thousand Diné people became prisoners at Fort Sumner from 1864 to 1868. The conditions were deplorable and unfit for habitation. The water contained alkali, crops failed miserably due to bad water and insect infestation, very little wood was available for cooking and heating, Comanche raids were common, sickness was rampant, disease spread rapidly, and depression disillusioned Diné people. Many died. The Fort Sumner reservation was a disaster. Diné people pleaded to return home, and the government took notice of the amount of money required to maintain it.

On June 1, 1868, a treaty was signed allowing the people to return to their homeland, and the U.S. Senate ratified it. This captivity experience convinced many Diné people to no longer take up arms to fight the U.S. military. Diné people wanted to stay in their homeland, and to ensure this, they would abide by the 1868 treaty, and they still do to this day. The horrible events and the inhuman treatment unified the Diné. For the next sixty years, Diné people strengthened. They grew their sheep and livestock herd, the population increased, the reservation land base increased, and the way of life thrived.

From 1868 to the 1930s, the people sustained their Diné identity. Only a few Diné children went to school during this period, even though a Western education was promised in the 1868 treaty. Most stayed home to raise sheep and livestock and to grow crops. Navajo communities expanded. American activities and sports such as basketball, rodeo, and fairs were introduced. The Northern Navajo Nation Fair in Shiprock started in 1911, and the Navajo Tribal Fair was established in 1937. These two events epitomized Diné identity. Diné people interacted socially, spoke Diné, and exercised their ceremonies.

In the late 1800s and early 1900s, Navajo leaders such as Henry "Chee" Dodge persuaded the federal government to increase the reservation land base. Thousands of acres were put into trust by presidential executive orders and congressional approval in 1878, 1880, 1882, 1884, 1886, 1900, 1901, 1905, 1907, 1913, 1918, 1930, and 1934. Dodge and others also requested from the federal government monies to help contribute to the rapid growth of livestock. This growth led to economic stability and to the rise in the number of trading posts on the reservation. The huge number of sheep and livestock also led to an increase in weaving production. Traders encouraged this rapid growth of sheep to increase trade volume, producing better financial results for non-Navajos. The Navajo economy and way of life are strongly interwoven with sheep raising and weaving.

The federal government maintained a paternalistic attitude toward Diné peoples. Problems arose, such as health care with the flu pandemic in 1918 and 1919. The people suffered racism and bias by non-Diné persisting throughout the twentieth century. The federal government's actions, however, led to the biggest impacts. Oil companies such as Midwest Refining Company, Western States Oil and Gas, and others wanted to search for oil on Native lands, and they pushed for the federal government to help them. In 1922, Midwest Refining Company won a 4,800-acre lease in the San Juan region of the reservation. Meanwhile, a centralized Navajo government did not exist. The U.S. government hired Herbert J. Hagerman to be a special commissioner charged with the responsibility of negotiating with the Diné people. Hagerman consequently established a tribal council, with twelve primary delegates and twelve alternate delegates. The tribal council's primary role was to approve leases to these oil companies. They had little power to do anything else, and they could only meet when Hagerman was present at the meetings. This "business council" started a Western government system.[19]

In conjunction with the establishment of a council, the federal government wanted to deal with overgrazing on the reservation. The livestock population had bloomed to roughly 1.5 million head by 1930.[20] Several times throughout the 1930s and 1940s, hundreds of horses, goats, and sheep died due to lack of food in the region.

John Collier, who became the commissioner of Indian affairs in 1933, consulted with non-Diné scientists to decide the best course of action. Diné families were not consulted. Non-Diné scientists told Collier only five hundred thousand head of livestock were suitable for the land.[21] The people were ordered to reduce their livestock. Livestock owners were forced to sell horses, goats, and finally ewe sheep. Many Diné families witnessed the killing of thousands of animals and consequently the decimation of their economy and way of life. Buck Austin, a Navajo sheepherder, tells of the destruction: "Those disturbances over stock reduction affected the entire reservation. Hundreds of men and women were arrested because they simply refused to limit their herds. We went through extreme hardship, hunger, thirst, being beaten by police, arrested and being thrown in jail at places far away from our homes."[22]

The federal government hired some Diné men to compensate for the lost; however, wage labor did not reconcile the lost income and way of life. Hundreds of Diné people had to leave the reservation to find work or became dependent on the U.S. government. The overgrazing did not stop; instead, it increased because families settled into one place rather than move between homes. People tried to hold onto their land, and the plant life in some areas died out.

In the 1940s, thousands of Diné men enlisted in the armed forces to fight for the United States in World War II. The Diné language was used as a secret code in the Pacific theater.[23] The language enabled the United States to win key battles in the Pacific in the war against Japan. When Diné men returned home, many went off to college or moved to cities to find work. The reservation did not have the industries and manufacturing plants in place for Diné men to remain at home. The reservation was economically disadvantaged.[24]

After World War II, changes rapidly occurred that influenced Diné identity. Thousands of children were sent to Bureau of Indian Affairs boarding schools and special education programs, such as the Adult Vocational Training Program. Many Diné political leaders viewed an American education as a way to overcome widespread poverty and to achieve greater self-sufficiency. The Navajo economy shifted away from livestock and agriculture to wage labor, primarily in cities and border towns near the reservation.

State governments finally recognized the Diné people as American citizens with voting rights when Diné were granted the right to vote in Arizona and New Mexico in 1948 and in Utah in 1953. An increasing number of Diné joined the Native American Church (NAC) in the 1940s and 1950s. NAC members use peyote in their ceremonies, and the Navajo Tribal Council outlawed peyote on the reservation in 1940. The law was repealed twenty-plus years later. Diné spirituality shifted away from a traditional standpoint to incorporate Christianity, NAC, and other worldviews. This shift continues with many Diné practicing some form of Christian denomination or NAC. Fewer Diné people follow traditional spirituality.[25]

The uranium industry in the United States boomed in the 1950s. From 1952 to 1963, Kerr-McGee operated uranium mines near Shiprock. Hundreds of Diné men worked in the mines.[26] Coal-mining operations began in the 1950s and 1960s, although they will end soon with many companies, states, and corporations moving toward renewable energies. The Navajo Generating Station in Page, Arizona, closed in December 2019. The oil industry provided millions of dollars to the tribal government. More Diné men sought jobs in these industries, but many of them got sick and died later from their work-related experiences. Many families never got compensated for their losses. Fewer and fewer Diné families raised livestock, and more and more were moving away from the reservation to border towns like Flagstaff, Arizona; Gallup, New Mexico; Farmington, New Mexico; and Page, Arizona. The push by the federal government to finally come up with an answer to the "Indian problem" led to the idea of terminating federal recognition of Native nations and relocating tribal citizens to urban environments. Diné people were not exempt. Many Diné moved to cities and acculturated to an American way of life by no longer maintaining tribal affiliation.

In 1966, Rough Rock, Arizona, became the first Native community to administer and control elementary and secondary education. In 1968, Navajo Community College opened in Tsaile, Arizona, and became the first Native American community college in the country.[27] Nevertheless, most schools on the reservation did not focus on teaching the Diné language and history until the 1990s.

In 1964 and again in 1966, the Navajo tribal government signed two leases with Peabody Coal Company to mine for coal at Black Mesa, Arizona. The lease in 1966 called for the company to pay twenty cents per ton for coal destined for the Navajo Generating Station in Page, Arizona, and twenty-five cents per ton for coal employed at more distant sites, such as the Mohave Generating Station at Bullhead City, Arizona.[28] Long-term damage to the water supply and the relocation of hundreds of Diné and some Hopi families resulted. Black Mesa Peabody Coal is no longer in operation after forty years. It closed in 2005.

Trading posts declined in the 1960s. More and more Diné families went to stores located in Farmington and Gallup, New Mexico, because prices were cheaper. The long-standing practice of going to the trader for services dissipated. More Diné families bought trucks and no longer relied on horses and wagons. Interactions with non-Diné in the border towns produced racial tensions and conflicts. Diné patrons experienced blatant racism, yet Diné residents continue to go to Gallup and Farmington for necessary services and goods. Other establishments opened up on the reservation, such as gas stations, restaurants, and retail outlets.

By 2011, the Navajo Nation had an enrollment of more than 300,000.[29] More than 150,000 live away from the reservation, mostly in border towns, such as Farmington and Gallup, and in cities such as Phoenix, Albuquerque, Tucson, Denver, Salt Lake City, and Los Angeles. The median age of the Navajo Nation is roughly between twenty and twenty-six. As more Diné become college educated, many move to cities for economic opportunities, not because of the collapse of identity. Most opportunities are in cities, and many Diné families no longer raise livestock. Many American families have also left farms behind to find work and opportunities in urban areas.

Diné women have always been strong individuals, with the power to determine the political and social well-being of Diné families and clans. Over the last one hundred years, Diné women have undergone difficult changes. Very few women are a part of the Navajo Nation Council; Christianity has lessened the power women had in the Diné spiritual realm; and Western values have restricted options and limited possibilities for political and social achievement and fulfillment.

Nonetheless, the majority of Diné college graduates are women, and the opportunities for women are expanding in the twenty-first century. With this shift in the status of women and their roles and responsibilities, Diné women are accomplishing many notable achievements. They are medical doctors, judges, lawyers, teachers, heads of households, political officials, police officers, professors, engineers, managers, and in other careers.

Diné baa hane' shows how even though the people have gone through changes, identity is continuously reinforced. The Navajo reservation is located between the four sacred mountains. Some Diné families continue to raise sheep and grow crops. Urban Diné communities have developed in Phoenix, Albuquerque, Denver, and Los Angeles. The Diné language continues to be spoken by thousands of people. Diné

Figure 2 Author making Diné kelchi (moccasin).

people living outside of Níhi Kéyah continue to travel back to visit parents, other relatives, and friends. Some Diné follow the philosophical principles of SNBH and hózhǫ́. Many Diné people have respect for their ancestors' tenacity to survive and persevere, making them proud of their identity. Diné identity continues.

TWO
Sạ'áh Naagháí Bik'eh Hózhǫǫn

The old man lifted his head and said, "Grandsons! Why would you kill me? I am dichin hastiih (hunger). How are people going to live in the future without me? Would you have them eating just one meal forever? There will be new food to eat and taste whenever people are hungry. People are born with openings for the taking in and giving out of food. Is that not so?"

"We will spare your life," said one of the twins. "I can see that you may be useful in the future. But here is another one we can kill," said the other twin. "Look at him. He is hideous old creature and surely must be a monster of destruction." "You cannot kill me, grandson," said this old man. "You must let me live for I am té'é'i hastiih (poverty). Clothes must be worn out. Moccasins must someday have holes in their soles. You see I can be useful. If old things did not wear out there would be no reason for making new ones."

—*NAVAJO HISTORY*, VOLUME I

Sạ'áh Naagháí Bik'eh Hózhǫǫn (SNBH) is Diné philosophy. Diné scholar Miranda Haskie, in "Preserving a Culture: Practicing the Navajo Principles of Hozho doo K'é," discusses how her grandfather, Albert "Chic" Sandoval, lived by the principles of k'é, hózhǫ, and SNBH: "In order to survive the integration with a dominant culture, the secondary culture must meet certain conditions. When these conditions are met, people successfully preserve their culture. These conditions include practicing Hózhǫ dóó K'é, becoming educated, utilizing tools (products of preservation, such as customs that have been recorded on tape and in books), practicing leadership, changing, and adapting."[1]

Sandoval was elected to the Navajo Tribal Council in 1928 and was an interpreter, linguist, and teacher of Navajo studies. He helped conduct research for the fields of anthropology, ethnology, education, health, and linguistics. Sandoval worked with numerous scholars, such as Robert Young, Father Berard Haile, Edward Sapir, Charlotte J. Frisbie, John Adair, Clifford Barnett, and David P. McAllester.

Diné people create tangible and intangible products reflecting SNBH. Some intangible items are songs, prayers, chants, and stories, and some tangible items are moccasins, dresses, jewelry, skirts, and pants. These items represent Diné identity as a living process. Whether a Diné individual chooses to write poetry, tell stories, go to college, become a surgeon, or help scholars research the language and culture, or chooses to herd sheep, grow crops, or learn cultural aspects later in life, the person is Diné.

SNBH has meanings and understandings for each human being. According to Haskie, SNBH is so powerful that when people "follow the path of SNBH, the natural teaching," we understand "the depth of our life."[2] She continues, "We will believe in ourselves, have trust in ourselves, believe in what we are doing and we will understand and know where we are going in this life." SNBH "represents the Diné traditional system of values and beliefs that provide teaching and learning of human existence in harmony with the natural world."[3]

SNBH is where a Diné person learns the teachings and achieves a healthy well-being in life.[4] SNBH is a planning and learning process central to a Diné way of knowing.[5] The planning and learning process is nitsáhákees (thinking), nahat'á (planning), iiná (living), and siihasin (reflecting). The process is comprehensive. In accordance with a Diné paradigm discussed in chapter 4, its order starts in the east and proceeds sunwise through the cardinal directions.[6] To comprehend SNBH is to realize wholeness and achieve completeness.[7]

SNBH administers a way of acknowledging and overcoming con-flicts, difficulties, chaos, and contradictions. SNBH accepts that unsettling forces and change are normal; they are present in life and experienced often in the past.[8] These conflicts and changes are witness to the upheavals and displacements in Diné history and embody the people's strength.

More than three hundred thousand people identify as Diné, and each person has his or her own individual outlook on life, beliefs, and aspirations.[9] American ideology and way of life has affected how Diné people think and live. Current Diné thought is fairly individualistic and less communal than it was two hundred years ago.

In a world where individualism has become a way of life for many Diné people, SNBH reflects space and time where a person's identity is tied to community. Without a community's well-being, the person does not achieve a sense of wellness.

One common meaning of SNBH is long life and happiness. It represents a principle embodied in a Diné person's life. Various Diné and non-Diné scholars have investigated SNBH's meaning, and each analysis focuses on each word. For instance, Gary Witherspoon probes the implicit meaning of each lexical item in *Language and Art in the Navajo Universe*. Linguist Robert Young and William Morgan, who developed the Navajo written language and language dictionary, considered the meaning of each word. The next several paragraphs provide a more holistic picture of a distinct Diné epistemology rather than an exploration of each lexical item.

SNBH comes from First Man and is a powerful paradigm. The Diyin Dineʼé instructed the people to live a SNBH path to ensure wellness, prosperity, and continuance. SNBH guides the people to believe and trust in their daily responsibilities. This belief and trust help the people understand and know by providing confidence in their decision-making processes. Some Diné people refer to SNBH as the corn pollen path (tádídíín bekʼeh eʼetiin). Corn pollen is an offering a person uses in their prayers and ceremonies. Corn pollen is life, security, and community.

SNBH is also known as Hózhóogo Iiná (Blessing Way) and Dahtoo' bikeh e'etiin (Way of Dew).[10] A Diné person following SNBH has strong family and community connections. For example, Hózhǫ́ǫ́jí (Blessing Way ceremony) is the backbone of Diné ceremonies. The ceremony is the most harmonious, peaceful, and happiest. The Blessing Way maintains and protects a person and helps establish tranquility for a person and community. SNBH guides a person and community to completeness.

SNBH represents an educational planning and learning process. Diné College follows SNBH in its vision, mission, and curriculum. As described above, the process has the following tenets: (1) nitsáhákees (thinking), (2) nahat'á (planning), (3) iiná (living), and (4) siihasin (reflecting). The process is where a person and community are unified and balanced. It is associated with the four cardinal directions (east, south, west, and north), the four sacred mountains (Mount Blanca, Mount Taylor, San Francisco Peaks, and Mount Hesperus), the four sacred minerals (white shell, turquoise, abalone, and black jet), the four parts of the day (dawn, day, sunset, and night), the four seasons of the year (fall, winter, spring, and summer), and the four life stages (birth, adolescence, adulthood, and old age). This planning and learning process helps to develop a Diné person's motivation and life goals. The passion to live and achieve is in SNBH.

SNBH is tied to multidimensional ways and interconnected realities. Life has energies, and the community and person have a responsibility to acknowledge and recognize these energies and apply them wisely in daily life. Energies exist in the universe. These forces are evident, and for a person and community to achieve well-being, the person and community strive for equilibrium and symmetry. In other words, moderation is the norm. Too much of the energies are harmful to the individual and community. All things are composed of halves of the whole; therefore, achieving wellness is to maintain equilibrium of the forces.

Each Diné person can understand SNBH in various ways. Traditionally, Diné people reached SNBH through land, cultural knowledge, trade, and sustainable living. Diné people do the same in the present, although exposure to various worldviews can make it challenging. Many Diné people do not fully understand SNBH, and those who do may only have surface knowledge. A small number of people, particularly hataałiis (healers) and those who know Diné ceremony, may have a comprehensive SNBH awareness.

Former Navajo Nation vice president Rex Lee Jim wrote on his journey to SNBH and how he came to realize what it meant for his life. His chapter "A Moment in My Life" in *Here First: Autobiographical Essays by Native American Writers* describes SNBH as a formula to empower him to design a life. His grasp of this formula is the following:

Giving order to these sounds and words empowers me to rise above and beyond myself. Words uplift me to heights from which I transform myself into a power that transmutes any experience into an energy, which I may direct toward a definite purpose that I desire to achieve. I am the maker of my destiny. From this height, I know that words, knowledge, thoughts, emotions, experiences are all important. Isolated and dormant, they are useless. They are potential power. What is more important is knowing how, when, and for what to use this power. Therein lies our personal power! From this height, everything matters. Everything matters![11]

Jim's grandfather taught him some knowledge of SNBH. He learned that it is the beauty of life realized through the application of teachings that work.[12] His essay starts with discussing the meaning of each word and then extends to include his own thoughts and experiences of Sạ'áh Naagháí Bik'eh Hózhǫ́ǫ́n nishlóo naasháadoo.

Literally, sa means old age, ah means beyond, naa means environment, ghái means movement, bi means to it, k'eh means according, hó means self and that sense of an ever-presence of something greater, zhóón means beauty, nishlóo means I will be, naasháa doo means I walk. This may be stated in the following way, "May I walk, being the omnipresent beauty created by the one that moves beyond old." Now we all know that we are born into this world and we live for some time and then we all die.[13]

Jim realizes that there is more to each word and its meaning beyond a simple definition. He says, "Suddenly sa no longer meant old age in terms of years; sa came to mean quality. Sa is quality. Quality of ever-improving spirituality, quality of physical growth, quality of social flexibility, and quality of mental processing."[14]

The exact meaning of SNBH is in the Diné language, yet the implementation is individual and communal. A person's well-being and happiness are interconnected to another person's well-being and all life on the earth. Diné people live their own individual lives yet are linked through their clans, nuclear and extended families, and communities. Jim equates this as "our responsible actions bring beauty into this world. This beauty comes about because of following the laws set forth by sa'ah naagháí. Fortunately, how sa'ah naagháí is formulated is within our complete control. By exercising this responsibility, we design our own lives. We bring beauty into this world. The beauty comes from within us. Hózhóón, then, is our inner self singing and dancing in the physical world."[15]

He meticulously reflects on how each word is translated through his own living and thought process. He says, "Acknowledgement and acceptance of ourselves the way we are, then, is also acknowledgement and acceptance of the gods. What the gods allow us is not to remain the way we are. The gods have endowed us with the power to transform ourselves into their own images, which ultimately reflects what we see as ideal, what we strive for."[16] His reflection and experience is one perspective.

In the following paragraphs, four Diné individuals share their views on SNBH. All their names have been changed to protect their identity. Jennifer Allison grew up on and off the reservation. She does not speak the Diné language proficiently; however, she knows enough to get by when she needs to. Her parents felt that it was best for her not to speak Diné and that the English language is more valuable. Jennifer spent most of her young life in boarding schools on and off the Navajo reservation. When she was young, she was embarrassed to be Diné and did not like her accent. She did not like herself because of the constant feeling her instructors projected, especially Christian instructors, that having brown skin and being Native was inferior. The pressure was also constant from dormitory parents and teachers at various schools she attended. One school she attended was on the East Coast. She was one of a few Native American students. She was alone quite a bit of the time, allowing her time to draw. She had been drawing since she was four. Art became an outlet for frustration, pain, and sadness. She had many difficult issues to struggle with in her young life, including self-esteem problems, domestic violence, and the birth of her son. During these difficult times, she attended Diné College. She earned an associate's degree in Navajo history and Indian studies, and the knowledge she gained helped her. She said, "Prayers are very important to me, they are a very, very strong part of my life. To be able to pray and to sing in my own language, and to be able to understand the philosophy behind my own language is very important. So everything I needed came from that and finding out who I am as a Navajo woman."[17]

Jennifer's Diné identity is focused on her spirituality. She says, "So for me, what it means to be Navajo is your relationship with your spirituality. I think that is the strongest part of being Navajo; whether that be Native American Church [NAC] or traditional, or whether that be Christian, or anything else. I know that is what it is to me."[18] Jennifer feels SNBH is the necessary balance for a Diné person, because without this balance, things in life are overwhelming and can be destructive. She experienced difficult identity issues, and realizing SNBH has benefited her. While Diné spirituality is a core part of her identity, she stresses that creating new traditions is also part of her identity: "The core values or the core philosophy of how you view the world, how you approach the world and walk in it and see yourself in the world is very important. . . . We need to continue to create Navajo culture, we need to continue to create new songs and new prayers[,] and that's where I'm going with my poetry and my artwork. My artwork is Navajo. My artwork is prayer."[19]

Her belief in creating new cultural traditions is tied to maintaining Diné identity. Jennifer is thinking on a different level, where SNBH allows the person to adapt to situations and lifeways while remaining connected to Diné knowledge. In other words, it is acceptable for a Diné person to use a computer, drive a car, speak English, and still be Diné because they live by SNBH. Jennifer is one who believes in living as you want and still being Diné at the core.

Adam Sims grew up on the Navajo reservation and spent some time in an urban environment. He attended public schools and does not speak the Diné language proficiently. He spent four years in the U.S. Marine Corps and graduated with a bachelor's degree. He lived on a farm with livestock and as a child heard traditional stories and played games, including késhjéé' (shoe game). Késhjéé' is played in the winter and involves two teams trying to guess which shoe has a ball hidden in it. The game represents a time when day and night animals played to determine whether the earth would be in daylight or night. Neither side won the game, so the earth has day and night.

Adam never questioned his Diné identity until college, where he took American Indian history courses and for the first time critically analyzed the Native condition. He now sees Diné identity in the following ways: (1) he wants to speak his language and know his way of life more; (2) he wants to get a good education and return home to help other Diné achieve a better life; (3) the environment shapes you as a person; and (4) he tries to follow a Diné way of life. Adam does not live on Níhi Kéyah, yet he is not disconnected from Diné identity and SNBH.

Tom Harris is a college graduate who grew up primarily in Albuquerque. He did not learn much about Diné way of life when he was young. His main exposure to Diné lifeways and language was through scolding or being told to do chores around the home. His teenage life was very different from how he lives as an adult. He tries to follow SNBH, and although he does not speak the Diné language, he is learning. He is also learning Diné narratives and how to think and live as a Diné man.

He is proud to be Diné. He says, "So being a Navajo, I try and look at everything in that perspective. I had to kind of pick it up and relearn a lot, the stories and stuff, and so my dependency on Western thought, white man's thought is slowly decreasing."[20] He is also learning about Diné cultural knowledge:

I was told that they call us Diné. I was told that we're actually called by another name, a traditional name and that name entails male and female warriors, that's what a definition of Navajo would be, that's why women when they were born[,] they were given warrior names. A lot of the women have the name Nana bah, Nez bah[;] those are female warrior names. Navajo is a man and female warrior[,] and according to that you have to be assertive in every aspect spiritually, mentally, physically, emotionally[,] and then you have to have compassion.[21]

Tom does not appear to have any difficulties balancing life. He does not believe a person—specifically, a Diné person—can live in two worlds.[22] He says:

I don't think it's possible to live in two worlds. I was always taught never to split yourself up[,] and how you're created[,] you have a clan [and] it should be a Navajo world[,] but so everything[,] even when you're involved with the western world[,] should be looked at as not necessarily or as a Navajo because the stuff you're not supposed to do are like the modern ways they have and everything[;] they have words for it in Navajo that you're not supposed to do, but it's still there, it exists, in a Navajo world too. I don't think it's possible to live in two worlds[;] the people who do that who try today, they have a hard time, when they say they're living in both worlds.[23]

He does not think a person can split themselves. He said Diné people who split into two worlds have difficulties. A Diné world is where the person lives by SNBH. They can drive a truck, work on the computer, watch Hollywood movies, eat hamburgers, and read Toni Morrison. In other words, a Diné person lives a balanced life. This balanced approach helps to overcome life's challenges.

Kim Jennings is a lawyer who worked for the Navajo Nation Department of Justice. She grew up on the Navajo reservation and in Tucson, Arizona. She did not learn the Diné language growing up. She attended mostly non-Diné and non-Native schools, but she also attended a law school with a support network for Native American law students.

Kim views her identity through her career. She is a lawyer who works for the Diné people. She says, "I think just that drive to protect it, itself means Navajo, that means you are a community, you stick together, you are descendants of the Holy People[,] and as such[,] you carry through with that as a group[;] no one person can decide for everyone[;] it's like a community decision, everything is a, there is [a] strong sense of comradery."[24] The need to protect the Navajo Nation and work for the Diné people is how Kim follows SNBH:

How I carry on with my life, is, it may seem simple, but you breath in and out the morning air, you walk outside, you exercise[.] I start the day like that and carry through the day, enjoying the sun, enjoying the day[,] and then once the day ends you return home and you just be thankful the day has gone the way it has[;] it could have been worse, say[,] like you might have had a bad day, but you always know that the next day is gonna be better or has to be better.[25]

Figure 3 Sheep corral of the author's aunt in Naschitti, New Mexico.

Kim lives a present-day lifestyle and strives to follow SNBH. That is not to say it has been easy, for she is still learning how to balance life, as all Diné are learning to do.

SNBH is a pathway for wellness and happiness. The individuals in this chapter are striving to live by SNBH. This learning process can take a whole lifetime; for others, it is learned sooner; although the experiences of wellness and happiness occur over one's lifetime. SNBH is experienced differently for each Diné person, although Diné knowledge is the same for all. SNBH is the beauty of a Diné way of life.

THREE
Diné Bizaad

The Navajo Nation has more than one hundred thousand fluent speakers, most of them bilingual in Diné and English.[1] The Diné language is vibrant, but concerns about its continuance remain. The number of monolingual Diné speakers is relegated to the older and middle generations. It is becoming a challenge to find a young person under the age of eighteen who is a monolingual Diné speaker. By far, the majority of young Diné people speak English. Consequently, individuals and communities are concerned about maintaining the Diné language. They rely on schools, colleges, and the tribal government for valuable guidance.

This chapter reviews how Diné bizaad (Diné language) created and guides the Diné world. Gary Witherspoon's *Language and Art in the Navajo Universe* is the primary source guiding this chapter. I also discuss Diné language shift and the implications of language vitality to the Navajo Nation.

Diné people have spoken Diné bizaad for generations. They speak the language, transmit cultural knowledge, interact with one another, and tell stories. They use the language to communicate with the Diyin Dine'é (Holy People). Diné bizaad is the people's distinctiveness.

Creating and Guiding the World Through Language

The Diyin Dine'é created the world the Diné people and all humans live in. They entered the sweathouse and thought the world into existence.[2] The Holy People's thoughts created speech, song, and prayer. Mary C. Wheelwright recorded the beginning of the world song, and Gary Witherspoon translated it.

First verse:

The earth will be,
The mountains will be,
[and so on, mentioning other things to be]

Second verse:

The earth will be, from ancient
times with me there is knowledge of it.
The mountains will be, from ancient
times with me there is knowledge of it.
[and so on]

Third verse:

The earth will be, from the very
beginning I have thought it.
The mountains will be, from the very
beginning I have thought it.
[and so on]

Fourth verse:

The earth will be, from ancient times
I speak it.

The mountains will be, from ancient times
I speak it.

[and so on]

Fifth verse:

[The fifth verse is a repetition of the first
verse, rendering the sense "and so it will be"
or "and thus it will be done."][3]

Leland Wyman recorded a similar song for his book *Blessingway*.

(1) Of Earth's origin I have full knowledge . . .
(2) I had full knowledge from the very beginning . . .
(3) Long ago he was thinking of it . . . of Earth's origin he was
thinking.[4]

Thought, song, speech, and prayer are the Diné language. Są'áh
Naagháí and Bik'eh Hózhǫǫn frame what the language is, the sacred-
ness and power. These two entities came from First Man's medicine
bundle, and they represent thought and speech, male and female.
Wyman writes:

"Of all these various kinds of holy ones that have been made, you the
first one will be (represent) their thought, you will be called Long Life
(Sa'ah Naaghai)," he was told. "And you who are the second one, of all
Holy People that are put to use first, you will be (represent) their speech,
you will be called Happiness (Bik'eh Hozho)," he was told. That much
so happened. "You will be (found) among everything (especially ceremonial affairs) without exception, exactly all will be long life by means
of you two, and exactly all will be happiness by means of you two," was
said to them.[5]

These two entities are the parents to Asdzą́ą́ Nádleehé (Changing Woman). Są'áh Naagháí and Bik'eh Hózhǫ́ are in Diné songs and prayers. They represent the ideal in life. The ideal in Diné life is to live to maturity in the condition described as hózhǫ́, and to die of old age, the end result of which incorporates one into the universal beauty, harmony, and happiness described as Są'áh Naagháí Bik'eh Hózhǫ́ǫ́n.[6] Są'áh Naagháí and Bik'eh Hózhǫ́ are animating powers in the universe, and they produce a world based on hózhǫ́. These two entities are the inner and outer forms of life. In Diné thought, all living beings have inner and outer forms, including the air, the mountains, and the earth. These two entities are the inner and outer forms and harmonize with each other. An example is the Blessing Way (Hózhǫ́ǫ́jí), a ceremony to restore order, beauty, happiness, and harmony to a person and the people. Witherspoon describes the Blessing Way song and prayer in the ceremony:

Earth's feet have become my feet
by means of these I shall live on.
Earth's legs have become my legs
by means of this I shall live on.
Earth's body has become my body
by means of this I shall live on.
Earth's mind has become my mind
by means of this I shall live on.
Earth's voice has become my voice
by means of this I shall live on.
Earth's headplume has become my headplume
by means of this I shall live on.
The cord-like extension from the top of its head
is cord-like from the top of my head
as by means of this I shall live on.
There are mountains encircling it and

Hózhó extends up their slopes,
by means of these it will be hózhó as I shall live on.
Są'áh Naagháí Bik'eh Hózhó I shall be,
Before me it will be hózhó as I live on,
Behind me it will be hózhó as I live on,
Below me it will be hózhó as I live on,
Above me it will be hózhó as I live on.
Hózhó has been restored.
Hózhó has been restored.
Hózhó has been restored.
Hózhó has been restored.[7]

The Diyin Dine'é sung this at the time of creation, and it has been passed down to the people. Diné thought emphasizes the importance of good thoughts, which will lead to good fortune and good things happening. The people believe thought is sacred and has power. The world was created by thought. In thought, things are created, and life is nourished. People are blessed and cured, and happiness is sustained and restored through this power.

Thought is paired with speech. Speech is the externalization of thought and also its extension. Speech has the same power as thought. With prayer and song, thought and speech are usually repeated four times.

Along with thought and speech, knowledge is a part of the creation of the world. Knowledge precedes and helps thought. Language is also a part of the creation of the world. Language precedes speech and is a primordial element in the universe. Knowledge is power, and the greatest power to transform or restore various ways comes from the knowledge of various ceremonies acquired from the Diyin Dine'é.

Knowledge is fixed because it comes from the Diyin Dine'é and the creation of the world. Humans can expand their awareness or command of knowledge but cannot increase it or add something not already developed. We can learn and communicate knowledge as well. We can create from knowledge as the Diyin Dine'é did. The Diyin Dine'é said, "We are planning to extend knowledge endlessly."[8] Knowledge, language, thought, and speech are based on action and ritual.

Diné ceremonies are designed to maintain or restore hózhǫ́. The opposite of hózhǫ́ is hóchxǫ́', which is disorder, badness, and things not beautiful. Diné ceremonies and rituals are based on how they maintain, ensure, or restore hózhǫ́. The first set are ceremonies that maintain and reinforce hózhǫ́; the second set focuses on transforming malevolent and dangerous powers into benevolent powers; and the third set of ceremonies exorcise the bad power of malevolent Diyin Dine'é to restore hózhǫ́. These ceremonies connect the Diyin Dine'é and the people.

Diné bizaad is an essential tool for this connection, and it is also a means of transforming chaos into cosmos and the reversal of cosmos to chaos. The language is part of the good and order as well as the bad and disorder. Both are intertwined, and language acknowledges this, yet good and order have the advantage. Language cannot be without knowledge, thought, and speech.

Symbols existed prior to language, knowledge, thought, and speech. They are the building blocks of mental thoughts and images. First Man and First Woman did not create symbols, yet they did originate the form in which to understand symbols. Gary Witherspoon describes how symbols preceded language, knowledge, thought, and speech in *Language and Art in the Navajo Universe.* "Knowledge is the awareness of symbol, thought is the organization of symbol, speech is the externalization of symbol, and compulsion is the realization of symbol. Symbol is word, and word is the means by which substance is organized and transformed. Both substance and symbol are primordial, for in the beginning were the word and the element, the symbol and the symbolized."[9]

Diné bizaad was used to create the world. It is sacred and has power. Diné healer Curtis Yanito explains this: "The Navajo language is unique because it is so connected to nature. Our words were given to us when everything was made. . . . Only pure Navajo words are used in the ceremonies. Navajo words can heal you. Just learning Navajo can heal you. It is nature speaking."[10] Yanito goes on to describe how his father was hit by a truck and received multiple injuries, including a broken neck, and was in a coma, paralyzed. A medicine man was called, and a prayer was done. Almost immediately Yanito's father was healed. He says, "My father's fingers moved. His toes moved. It was really amazing. . . . He (later) walked out of the hospital with a whole body. Even his broken neck healed."[11]

The Diné language is active and static energy. The language reflects movement and action. A Diné person is a human being when the person masters the art of speaking the language. Language, thought, speech, and knowledge are active, and this motion and process has a source of power: air.

In the world, air is the only entity with the capacity to move and bear knowledge. Air is a source of thought for humans. Air helped create and guide the world. It also the source of life for plants and animals. Air has great power for life and motion. Without air, many living things do not function. For example, fire is needed for cooking and heating and is dependent on air. Fire would cease to exist without air.

Diné people and all human beings need air to live. Breathing for humans is a part of our motion and soul. The following excerpt describes this understanding: "White wind gave his daughter and her son part of his breath, just as a man teaches his son or his sister's son prayers and songs and they become his; or as a father or mother may give their daughter and son advice and instruction. . . . He became their soul without diminishing himself, and gave them movement and life."[12]

Speech and sound occur with air. Diné people view speech as a sacred and powerful act, and one must properly and appropriately speak well. With speech, a person can guide and compel behavior and replicate the power of the Diyin Dine'é. Air is the ultimate source of hózhó because it is the source of life and motion. Since air is the ultimate source of life and connects all things, humans participate in this power and order through breath, thought, and speech. Humans harmonize the blessedness of the environment and restore this blessedness through language. Without language, humans are an inactive part of the universe, where they do not find meaning for life. With language, humans are an active, creative, and powerful entity in the universe. Language helps humans understand and find meaning in life and helps create and express it. Language classifies the world through relations, gender, and sexuality. K'é and k'éí frame Diné relations. In chapter 4 I discuss the two in more detail. In the following paragraphs, both are discussed in terms of gender, sexuality, and relations. K'é refers to affectionate action in the concepts of love, compassion, kindness, friendliness, generosity, and peacefulness. Diné people live love, compassion, kindness, friendliness, generosity, and peacefulness and do not merely speak about it. K'é is the Diné understanding of reproduction. It is understood regarding the giving and sustaining of life and procreating. The mother-child bond characterizes the nurturing and sustaining of life through sharing items of sustenance. It is powerful and intense and is the most enduring bond to be considered among the people as an ideal pattern for all social interaction. This mother-child bond replicates reciprocity and expresses the affective action of sharing sustenance. In contrast, the husband-wife bond characterizes mating, but it is not the same as the mother-child bond.

K'é is an act of giving life and sharing sustenance and signifies a relationship bond and behavioral code for humans. The language reflects different bonds. For instance, the word *shimá* refers to mother in a biological, social, clan, and family way. The people never refer to the individual by the person's first or last name but always through this bond system, because it is the proper and respectful way of social interaction. The use of first or last names distances the individuals and does not create a sense of love, compassion, friendliness, generosity, and peacefulness.

K'é does not emphasize independence, self-reliance, and separateness; rather, people connect themselves to all entities in this world. This relation creates a bond in which the individual understands that they are not alone and have family in places. It also shows the love and peacefulness humans seek and want. Fulfillment comes from the social and affective acts and bonds, which helps the person unite and harmonize with the social universe.

K'é is a relations system of good will and peacefulness. It is through good will and peacefulness that the people create harmony, balance, and order. It reduces the prospect of bad or ill will in the world. Good will and peacefulness are constant in life, and k'é mirrors this way. The world is based on the concept of k'é, and the language classifies it. For example, the word *shimá* refers to one's birth mother and also the earth, the sheep herd, the cornfield, and the mountain bundle. The reference to other things in the world creates a social bond between humans and all entities. This bond is reciprocity. It is the sustaining of life through sharing items of sustenance. Humans cannot live without the earth. The sheep herd, cornfield, and mountain bundle help the people maintain wellness. A mountain bundle is a collection of items such as earth from the sacred mountains. K'é grounds the people to each other and all living entities on the earth and in the universe.

K'éí is based on the components of gender, generation, age, and descent. The primary Diné descent system is clanship. The Diné clan system is defined through the: (1) mother's clan; (2) father's clan; (3) mother's father's clan (mother's born-for clan); and (4) father's father's clan (father's born-for clan). Every Diné child is their mother's clan. The child is "born for" their father's clan. The child is related to the clans for which the mother and father are born (clans of mother's father and father's father). More than sixty clans represent Diné descent and ana'í (alien) groups as well.

Because Diné persons are family based on the same or related clans, certain terminologies apply; for instance, all female of a man's clan are shimá, and all male of a man's clan are shik'is. The person's father's clan is referred to as shizhé'é. The terms show where people are in a family system. It is designed to reveal whom a person can love and marry.

Diné persons are forbidden to be in a sexual relationship with or marry a person who is of the same or related clans. In fact, when marriages were arranged, the first question asked during the negotiation was the person's clans. If they were not the same or related, then the marriage could take place. If they were the same or related, then a marriage could not happen.

Along with marriage, gender is linked to language. Life is synthesized through the concepts of maleness and femaleness. Actually, all of life is constructed through male and female traits. Maleness is associated with static dimensions of reality, and femaleness is associated with active dimensions. The female is active, productive, and reproductive. The capacity to create or reproduce life is inherent in the female, and to sustain life and produce food is also associated with the female.

Most ceremonial practitioners are men because the ritual and ceremonial domain is associated with thought and with maleness. Social and economic life is associated with femaleness because of movement, change, activity, and productivity. Maleness is associated with origins and culmination of things, and femaleness with growth, process, and change. Directions and the pathway of the sun are also categorized as male and female. For instance, east, the beginning of the day and direction, and north, the end of the day and darkness are male. South, the daylight period, and west, with evening twilight, are female. The sky is male, and the earth is female.

These constructs show the interrelatedness of the world and how k'é and k'éí emphasize the social bonding and interconnectedness based on the concepts of love, compassion, generosity, friendliness, and peacefulness. The balance between male and female is exercised through the language.

Diné bizaad created the world and guides the Diné people. One of the consequences of American colonialism is language shift, where a majority of Diné children speak English first, and Diné bizaad is spoken less.

Language Shift

Many Diné children in the twenty-first century do not speak Diné bizaad, although many regard it as important to identity. Some are in the process of learning the language, and a few communities are attempting to revitalize it.

Language is pivotal because a Diné way of life, including knowledge, prayers, songs, ceremonies, rituals, and stories, is based on how a person interprets, analyzes, and synthesizes it through the language. Studies by Wayne Holm, Paul Platero, Evangeline Parsons-Yazzie, Tiffany S. Lee, Teresa L. McCarty, Deborah House, and several others confirm Diné language shift. Joshua A. Fishman's *Reversing Language Shift*; James Crawford's "Endangered Native American Languages: What Is to Be Done, and Why?"; Teresa L. McCarty, Mary Eunice Romero-Little, and Ofelia Zepeda's "Native American Youth Discourses on Language Shift and Retention: Ideological Cross-Currents and their Implications for Language Planning"; and numerous other articles and studies have documented language shift in many Indigenous communities throughout the world.[13] Even with language shift, several Indigenous communities, such as the Wampanoag, Cherokee, and Hawaiian, see how critical language is to their identity. The following individuals discuss how language is Diné identity. The names have been changed to protect their privacy.

Tom Jones sees his identity through his ability to speak Diné. For Tom, speaking a Native language is what makes an Indigenous person Indigenous. "I would define being Navajo as knowing where you come from, knowing your language, knowing the Navajo teachings, and having that identification of growing up on the reservation with the livestock, your parents teaching you the ways of the Navajo traditions, where the Navajo comes from and how we got to be where we are."[14]

Language is core. Many Native communities are attempting to revitalize and maintain their Native languages. It is a challenge, but success stories are happening in Hawaii and among the Maori in New Zealand, the Wampanoag in Massachusetts, and in other Native communities.

Tom notes that early in his life, he was ashamed of his identity and family. He says, "At one point, I remember I didn't want to be Navajo and that was because I was embarrassed of the kind of lifestyle and the kind of dysfunctional family that I was raised [in] in comparison to other [non-Native] families that I had met while growing up."[15] Native individuals feeling ashamed of their identity is not unusual. They try to conceal it because they do not have certain material goods, such as a computer or other items distinguishing socioeconomic status; or because they do not have a job or a college education, or have family members who are alcoholics; or because they are ashamed of their living condition or many other conditions affecting life. Tom realizes the importance of language to his identity, and it has helped him overcome this initial feeling.

Steve Thomas does not speak Diné bizaad proficiently, but he spent quite a bit of time on the reservation living with his grandmother. He says, "One of the reasons I always went out to the rez [was] because she wanted me to know who I was and know where I came from and learn the language and culture. Back in high school I kind of threw it upon myself to do that, to go through and try to study my language, history of the Navajo people, and also the culture and spirituality."[16] Although Steve did not learn to speak Diné during his time with his grandmother, he feels the language is his identity. He views himself as Diné and is learning Diné bizaad. "I'm always trying to learn more about my identity, like language, culture. That's how I pass my day-to-day life. I'm always looking at books that come out on the story of the Diné people. I always look through them and see what they write about and see what's in there and look at the pictures and also talk to other Navajos, friends, and also my mom too. I ask her questions now and then."[17]

He converses with other Diné of his generation about the history and way of life. Steve believes many Diné people of his generation have much in common, and Diné identity is strong. In his personal pursuit to learn the language, he links identity with language and way of life. He notes, "I think a common theme is holding onto the language, making sure that as a Navajo, you should know your language and culture, and that's something that shouldn't die out."[18] Steve is making an effort to learn to speak the language and is helping to revitalize it. He is living his own life yet is connected to Diné people and way of life.

Language shift is a reality for the Diné people. During the 2014 Navajo Nation presidential election, candidate Chris Deschene was disqualified because he did not take an exam to determine his language status. In July 2015, the Diné people voted to change the requirement for presidential and vice presidential candidates. In the future, presidential candidates will need to speak and understand the Navajo and English languages, and this ability shall be determined by the Navajo voters when they cast a ballot.[19] While knowledge of the language is still required to be president or vice president, the people, rather than the Navajo Election Administration, determine the requirement with their vote. The future of the language rests with the people.

Conclusion

Diné bizaad created and guides the world. It is a cornerstone to Diné identity. A Diné way of life is interwoven with the language, which is vital to living, transmitting, and communicating Diné.

While the language is part of the foundation of Diné identity, language shift is a reality. The majority of Diné children are speaking English as their first language and in many cases English only. While the majority of Diné people view the language as important, American colonialism has severely affected all Diné communities and the people. These effects have enormous implications for the future of the language and Diné identity.

One implication is the probability of a Navajo Nation president not being a proficient Diné speaker. A second implication is that fewer ceremonies and rituals will be conducted in Diné bizaad, with English being used more often. A third implication is that only certain Diné communities will use the language in ceremonies and everyday activities. A fourth implication is that the government may emphasize the importance of language and authorize language immersion programs and other activities to help maintain and revitalize the language. A fifth

Figure 4 Navajo Nation flag.

implication is that the Diné people will survive and work to ensure that their identity, language, and way of life continues.

For hundreds of years, Diné people have sustained their way of life. They had to deal with many challenges, including Spanish encroachment, Mexican settlement, and an American invasion. They were removed to Bosque Redondo, but they were later able to return home.

The U.S. federal government destroyed self-sufficiency for many families with livestock reduction in the 1930s and 1940s, yet the people and way of life continue in the twenty-first century.

Reflecting on the past two hundred years, Diné people have faced many challenges, yet they persist in maintaining their identity and language. Although fewer medicine peoples are learning and engaging in Diné ceremonialism, and this has had an effect on language, the people realize this, and the Navajo Nation has instituted an apprentice program to help train Diné individuals to become healers and chanters. The future will be full of challenges for the Diné people; however, people are working hard to ensure the language is revitalized and sustained.

FOUR
K'é and K'éí

I n Diné, family consists of the nuclear family unit, the extended family unit, clans, and relations with the earth. This family structure is known as k'é, a daily presence for each person. It reinforces respect, kindness, cooperation, friendliness, reciprocity, and love.[1]

K'éí is clan relatives. While Diné who are related through clans are not biologically brothers, sisters, mothers, and fathers, they are clan brothers, clan sisters, clan mothers, and clan fathers. They are family. For example, Lori Arviso Alvord, in *The Scalpel and the Silver Bear*, explains her clans: "If you were Navajo, I would introduce myself to you by telling you my clans. My father's mother clan is Tsinaajinii, the black-streak wood clan; his father's clan is 'Ashiihi Diné'e, the salt clan. This would tell you not only where I come from but whether I am your 'sister,' because frequently in the Navajo world there are people around who may be one's relatives."[2]

In conjunction with hózhǫ, k'é and k'éí frame the Diné view of the universe as a web of relations. K'é and k'éí are fundamental to the Diné order of the earth and universe. With k'é, the people know how to properly conduct themselves toward each human being and to all beings in life. For example, a protocol including offerings and prayers must be followed to acquire herbs and plants. Herbs, plants, and animals provide the Diné people with food, ceremonial paraphernalia, and medicine. The people cannot take more than they should, for if the person or people do so, irresponsible destruction, overharvesting, and polluting will occur.

Diné children learn about their clan, the history, and etiquettes to ensure acceptable bounds of behavior toward relatives and other people. Children are instructed to use family terms when addressing parents, grandparents, siblings, aunts, uncles, cousins, and relatives of related clans. The people are also taught to use family terms when addressing any elderly person, even if they are not related, such as shimá for mother and shizhé'é for father. K'é gives, shares, and supports clan and nonclan relatives.

K'éí is descent and relations. In Diné, the child takes the clan of the mother, so the mother's clan is the primary identifier. The child's father's clan is secondary and is called the "born for" clan. Two other clans complete the clan family system, the maternal grandfather's clan and the paternal grandfather's clan. These clans establish grandparent-grandchild ties and help when a grandchild pursues cultural knowledge. When people share one or more of the four clans, the group composes a shik'éí (my relatives), a family connection is established, and people address each other in the proper way. Each Diné person will have numerous relatives.

The people are expected to contribute to the well-being and support of relatives, particularly the mother's clan. A person shares, gives, and provides emotional, psychological, physical, and spiritual support. When a clan relative comes to visit, the person or family is supposed to provide shelter and food. K'é also plays a significant role in ceremonies, where many people are needed to ensure that the ceremony goes well and is successful.

In political affairs, leaders were knowledgeable and skilled in k'é and other customary practices. The people chose and followed their leaders (naat'áanii). A leader's authority and power came from the trust the people had for the person. A leader was selected based on speaking ability, wisdom, spirituality, and the ability to guide the people and plan for the future. Leadership was for life, as long as the person held the people's confidence. Peacemaking was one of the main leadership services. Leaders resolved disputes. When issues came up, leaders discussed with the parties involved, and a solution was reached through consensus. To achieve consensus, leaders had to know k'é. Leaders had to show respect, kindness, cooperation, and friendliness, as well as use the proper family terms when addressing or talking with individuals.

Traditional Diné leadership came in two forms: hózhǫ́ójí naat'ááh (peace leaders) and hashkééjí naat'ááh (war leaders). A person could not be a peace and a war leader at the same time. They needed to live by example and follow two values, recognition and credibility. The person was recognized to be a good orator who was wise and fair. The leader helped the people overcome challenges and plan for the community's future.

Diné leadership worked hard to ensure tranquility and wellness in the community through egalitarianism. Everyone in the community participated in democracy. To achieve egalitarianism in Diné communities, hózhǫ́ must be met. Hózhǫ́ is a condition of peace, happiness, and completeness. When disputes occur in communities, the resolution to ensure the condition of hózhǫ́ comes through peacemaking. Diné peacemaking is a restorative justice system. In this judicial system, relationships are used to decide matters and to reject force and coercion. All the participants have an equal voice, and there is no single all-powerful decision maker, such as a judge in a retaliatory justice system. Children are also considered equal to adults in certain situations, such as the right to own property and to make decisions.

K'éí helps establish identity; determines clan relatives; shows responsibilities, duties, and obligations among clan relatives; and establishes the bounds of proper behavior among unrelated individuals and with non-Diné peoples.[3] The people share their resources with their clan relatives as a means of sustenance and spiritual and emotional support. This sharing and caring are expressions of love or to help a relative in need. They are reciprocated. Clan relatives will help one another when needed and not necessarily immediately.

Diné people use the same family terms biological relatives use to address each other. This helps the people stay connected and keeps the social system intact and meaningful. It acknowledges the respect and love a person has to their relatives and the people. Some of the family terms a person will use to address nonbiological members of their matrilineal clan are as follows: (1) members of one's generation are brother and sister, with the appropriate term for younger and older siblings used; (2) females of the mother's generation are mother or older sister if older or younger sister if younger; (3) males of the mother's generation are older brother if older or younger brother if younger (a female can also call a male of the mother's generation "my son"); (4) females of the grandmother's generation are mother or older sister; (5) males of the grandmother's generation are older brother (a female can also call a male of grandmother's generation "my son"); (6) a male will call the female member of his children's generation mother or younger sister and the male members younger brother or nephew; and (7) a female will call the male members of her generation son and the female members daughter, but she can also call them younger brother and younger sister.[4] This family system becomes more complex when you add the person's father's clan, maternal grandfather's clan, and paternal grandfather's clan.

The maternal clan and the born-for clan are pillars in k'éí. In the father's clan, the males of the born-for clan are usually called shizhé'é or shizhé'é yázhí (father's brother); the females are usually shimá or shimá yázhí (father's sister); and on some occasions, both are called shibizhi (reference to father's siblings). Born-for clan relatives may occasionally help with various ceremonies or family functions, and a father who is a hataałii (healer) may select one or more of his children as his apprentice.

The person's paternal and maternal grandfather clans are relatives and addressed as grandmother or grandfather without reference to age or generation. The family terms are applied to both biological and non-biological relatives in the paternal and maternal clan categories: maternal grandfather is shicheii; maternal grandmother is shimásáni; paternal grandfather is shinálí hastiin; and paternal grandmother is shinálí asdzáán.[5] The maternal grandparents usually taught etiquette, history, creation and journey narratives, and spirituality to their grandchildren.

Blood quantum does not equate to k'éí. Under a traditional system, a person who has a matrilineal clan is Diné even though they may possess a negligible amount of Diné blood. This is in sharp contradiction to the standard enrollment criteria of the Navajo Nation, which requires one-fourth degree Navajo blood to enroll and be a descendant of a relative based on the 1940 census roll. The mother's clan is the primary clan, and if the child's mother is Diné, then the child is Diné under the traditional system.

If the person has a non-Diné mother and a Diné father, then the person's born-for clan is the link to Diné identity, but under the clan system, the clan and identity will disappear with the person's grandchildren if the person's children marry non-Diné.[6] The grandchild might have less than the one-quarter blood quantum requirement and therefore be ineligible to enroll in the Navajo Nation. Under k'éí, however, even if the person has less Navajo blood, he or she is Diné if the mother is Diné.

Diné has a history of heterogeneity, since several clans trace their roots to surrounding Native communities, such as Zuni Pueblo, Jemez Pueblo, Hopi, Ute, and Apache. This diverse heritage, however, is not recognized by the enrollment criteria because of the one-quarter blood quantum requirement. The Navajo Nation government does not use k'éí in its enrollment criteria, but from a cultural perspective, k'éí is recognized. K'éí frames the customs and rules for family and Diné identity. The standards of enrollment are different criteria. The history of Diné biological heterogeneity is ignored. People who are ineligible under the current enrollment system are excluded for the failure to meet the racial standard. A Western government standard regulates internal and core Navajo affairs, which is inconsistent with the spirit of Diné fundamental law.[7]

K'éí frames the customs and rules for marriage, property, duties, and responsibilities in the family and community. In marriage, Diné persons are prohibited from marrying anyone who is the same mother's clan, father's clan, maternal grandfather's clan, paternal grandfather's clan, and related clans. If a Diné person marries someone who is the same or related clan, it is considered incest. Incest is associated with hóchx̨ǫ́', bad energy. Diné people do not necessarily want to be accused of hóchx̨ǫ́'. Traditionally, any person who married a clan relative was the subject of widespread ridicule.

The Navajo government twice prohibited clan relative marriage in 1993 and in 2005. The prohibition is found in Title 9 of the Navajo Nation Code:

§ 2. Plural marriage void

B. Marriage between parents and children, including grandparents and grandchildren of every degree, between brothers and sisters of one-half degree, as well as whole blood, and between uncles and nieces, aunts and nephews and between first cousins, is prohibited and void.[8]

§ 5. Requirement generally

In order to contract a Navajo Nation marriage, the following requirements must be fulfilled:

D. Parties who are Navajo Nation members, or who are eligible for enrollment, may not be of the same maternal clan or biological paternal clan. The provisions of this Subsection shall not affect the validity of any marriages legally contracted and validated under prior law.

E. Parties may not be related within the third degree of affinity. The provisions of this Subsection shall not affect the validity of any marriage legally contracted and validated under prior law.[9]

The law does not state the maternal and paternal grandfather's clans. It only states the biological maternal and paternal clans. From a legal standpoint, one can argue that marriage between individuals who are in the same or related through their maternal and/or paternal grandfather's clan is legal and therefore binding. From a traditional standpoint, however, the people would not approve of marriage into the maternal or paternal grandfathers' clans.

Traditionally, the maternal uncle was responsible for disciplining and instructing his nephews and nieces on life skills and activities related to sustenance and survival. This included the maternal uncle, who arranged and approved of the marriage of his nephews. When he found a suitable woman from an acceptable family for his nephew, he discussed the marriage proposal with the spouse's family, and if agreed, the amount of dowry was set. Marriage discussion usually occurred without the presence of the potential couple. A traditional marriage is really an agreement between two families and not between two individuals. The interest was in the community, family, and clan and not in the individual rights or preferences of the groom and bride.

A traditional wedding ceremony is a spiritual and a social event attended by the couple's families, relatives, and friends. The traditional wedding ceremony continues into the twenty-first century, although more and more families include a Christian church wedding or choose one type of wedding ceremony only. The traditional wedding usually takes place late afternoon or in the evening and at the bride's family residence. The ceremony is usually short, but after the ceremony is complete, relatives offer advice on a long and fulfilling marriage. The advice and discussion can take some time depending on the family and how many people speak. Eating and celebration happens afterward. This ceremony seeks the blessings of the Holy People so that the married couple will start life together in harmony with Diné bi'í'ool'į́į́ł (Diné way of life). The ceremony also links past generations with present and future generations.

Traditionally, a wedding ceremony is never questioned because the couple's clanship and families have been identified, and both families and relatives validate the ceremonial union. The husband also moves close to his wife's family's residence, although in the twenty-first century, other circumstances apply, such as a job, school, and other conveniences. The husband is now a contributing member of his wife's family and is known as nihaadaani (male in-law); the wife is nihizháá' áád (female in-law) to her husband's family.

In a traditional divorce, the husband usually left with only his personal belongings and moved back to his mother's residence. Most of the marital property, including livestock, farming equipment, and household items, remained with the wife for her and the children's support. Usually the children stayed with the mother as well. Notably, these rules are not necessarily the prevailing laws in the Navajo Nation court system.

Regarding property, traditional ownership is in three broad categories: community, family, and individual. Community resources include common water uses for domestic matters and livestock. Family refers to property owned and used in common by all members of the extended family, which may include matrilineal grandparents, aunts, uncles, cousins, siblings, and parents. Family property can also include farm and rangelands, fruit trees, farm produce, livestock, corrals, ceremonial hogan, equipment, and resources such as wells and water tanks. Individual property includes personal items such as clothing, saddles, ceremonial paraphernalia, and personally owned livestock such as horses. Other individual properties might be sacred words, knowledge of traditional stories, knowledge of herbs and plants, and other items. Some personal items will be buried with the individual, but it is common to see the elderly designate certain personal items to certain individuals in the family.

Diné people learn duties and responsibilities through k'éí. They are taught at an early age about their obligations within an extensive clanship network. Along with learning about their duties and responsibilities, they are taught about the Diné knowledge paradigm. The paradigm is framed in the cardinal directions. East is associated with light, the color white, and the sacred mountain Mount Blanca. South is associated with water, the color turquoise, and the sacred mountain Mount Taylor.

West is associated with air, the color yellow, and the sacred mountain San Francisco Peaks. North is associated with dirt, the color black, and the sacred mountain Mount Hesperus. Four learning methods are also tied to this knowledge paradigm. Nitsáhákees is thought and associated with east. Nahat'á is planning and associated with south. Iiná is living and associated with west. Siihasin is reflection and associated with north. The clans are also tied to the paradigm. The maternal clan teaches the child nitsáhákees and is associated with east. The father's clan teaches the child nahat'á and is associated with south. The maternal grandfather's clan teaches the child iiná and is associated with west; and the paternal grandfather's clan teaches the child siihasin and is associated with north. This knowledge teaches each Diné person the duties, responsibilities, and obligations based on family and clan.

K'é and k'éí are closely related but also distinctive. K'é is relations and interactions with positive values, and k'éí focuses on clan relatives and regulates domestic relations, including marriage, divorce, and property. Carol Shorty, John Morgan, and Joann Thompson discuss k'é and k'éí. The names have been changed to protect their identity.

Carol Shorty

Carol Shorty is a college graduate who attended Southwestern Indian Polytechnic Institute and the University of New Mexico. She did not grow up on the Navajo reservation. She speaks some Diné and knows how to write and read in Diné. She is Diné and Oneida. Carol is of the Turtle clan and born for Kinyaa'áanii. She cited family relations as the source of her sense of identity. For her, being of mixed heritage and belonging to two Native nations makes her understanding of family especially key. More and more Diné people are of mixed heritages.

Carol spent much of her time growing up with Diné aunts, uncles, cousins, and other relatives. She grew up in an apartment with five cousins, and she considered all of them sisters or brothers. Religion was also an influence in her early life. She attended the Reorganized Church of Jesus Christ of Latter-Day Saints. She spent time with her cousins, aunts, and uncles at events such as cultural ceremonies. Throughout this time, she did not speak Diné bizaad. She says, "At that time I didn't know a lot of Navajo, and I didn't read and write it, and so a lot of the older people, my aunts and uncles, came down on me, and so I never completely used it so I wasn't familiar with it."[10]

She married a non-Diné and has three children. She described her husband's family as different to her experience because her husband saw his family as only himself, Carol, and their three children. In other words, her husband saw only his nuclear family unit as family and not the extended relatives. Carol believes Native identity is tied to your extended family. She states, "I think being an Indian you have more of a connection to more than just you're immediate family, more than just your family but where you come from, where your family lives, and why they live there."[11]

Carol believes k'é is a pivotal indicator of who is Diné and who is not. She explains, "I think just in my appearance, I'm not the stereotypical Navajo. At first it kind of confuses people, but once I know someone's Navajo, and I think the thing that helps me connect is I know my clans and am able to understand the relationships, cause I think that every time I talk to a Navajo that's one of the big things is, do you know who you are?"[12] Diné people see connections to relatives as an important marker. Carol reaffirms this:

> I think what it means to be Navajo is going back to what it means to be who you are, where you come from, who your family is, what's your relationship with other Navajos. I think that's the biggest part because that makes you what you are today, and it's not going out herding sheep, butchering sheep, and sleeping on sheepskin rugs, or weaving in a hogan. It doesn't break down by where you live or being able to pass down your family history to your kids. That's the important thing, that you also let your kids know who they are.[13]

Carol sees family as fundamental to Diné identity. She knows life is challenging, and the love of family helps overcome it. Carol loves her family. Her family and relatives protect her and contribute to her well-being. She ensures the connection to family is sustained.

John Morgan

John Morgan, Táchii'nii and born for Tsi'naajinii, is a high school teacher who attended Haskell Junior College, Dana Lutheran College, and graduated with a bachelor's degree from Fort Lewis College. He grew up in the checkerboard region of the Navajo reservation in New Mexico. The checkerboard region is land not officially sanctioned as a federal reservation. Non-Diné and Diné people, mostly farmers and ranchers, live side by side with one another in the checkerboard region. He spent seven years away from home while attending the various colleges.

John speaks Diné bizaad fluently, and his family is the foundation of his identity. John's experience growing up was different from that of his parents particularly. John's father did not graduate from high school, and his mother graduated with a high school diploma. His parents' lives were challenging, but they provided a stable home environment. John says, "They had to take care of each other, their siblings, whether if they got an education or not, and then compare that to how I grew up. They provided a house for me; they provided almost everything, food on the table every evening for me, and they provided me a home and good living environment."[14] John acknowledges his different life experience from that of his parents, yet their home had a positive impact on him.

John is proud to be Diné and respects the clan system. His father taught him how to respect his elders and how to properly address them. John says, "He always taught his kids how to respect elders, and how to introduce yourself when you talk to an elder and so forth, and how to use your language because that was a very important weapon, you know, we could use and just be able to communicate with our elders."[15]

John believes a Diné person is Diné through their clans. He acknowledges k'éí represents Diné identity and way of life. He explains:

You are a person with a rare background, which people are losing because I notice even with these kids today, when they hit high school, you ask them what clan are you and they don't know their clans; they're losing their identity, basically. So to be Navajo today I think you have to really know who you are, define yourself where you come from, your cheii [maternal grandfather] and your grandmas are really from because that's who we are, and I used to remember my mom always used to say, even if you go to school up in Nebraska, your umbilical cord is still buried here in the sheep coral, so you're from here no matter what. So I think the people today need to find out where they're really from.[16]

John's parents' teachings helped him establish his values and identity.

Joann Thompson

Joann Thompson is Tábąąhá and born for Hooghanłaní. Her maternal grandfather is Ta'neeszahnii and paternal grandfather is Áshįįhí. Joann, a college graduate working for the U.S. Department of Justice, grew up on the Navajo reservation yet spent time at a Catholic boarding school from age twelve until her high school graduation. She is not proficient in Diné bizaad, even though her first language is Diné. She speaks mostly English, but was reintroduced to Diné bizaad in middle school. When Joann is with her parents, her parents speak Diné to her, and she responds in English.

Joann is an independent woman. Diné women are highly regarded for their strength, courage, and self-sufficiency. They are considered the family cornerstone and represent a strong people.

Joann sees her identity through her extended family. Even though she does not have any biological children, she is a mother in her extended family. She is a mother to her nephew. She acknowledges her nephew as her son, and he reciprocates this relationship. She says, "So that has, that always tickles me when I remember that because a lot of people always say, my gosh, you have a big family, and I say to them, well, they're all considered your brothers and your sisters, you know, and now their kids are considered your kids."[17]

She acknowledges that a Diné person must remember where they come from, must know their community, must carry on the cultural ways, always be generous, try to live in a good way (hózhǫ́ǫ́go naashaadóó dooleeł), and appreciate the history of the Diné people. She advocates "to acknowledge the past, the ways and practices to carry on, but also be very generous and try to live your life in a good way to reach that harmony, and always remember where it is you come from."[18] She connects with Diné people via family, clan, and community. Even though she works more than a thousand miles away from the Navajo Nation, she acknowledges her Diné identity through her family relations, particularly her responsibility as a mother to her nephew.

K'é and k'éí allow Diné people to be connected to one another, the earth, and the universe. The individuals in this section specifically mention family as Diné identity.

Conclusion

The laws underlying Diné domestic relations are called Yoołgaii Asdzáán Bibee Haz'áanii (Changing Woman's Law). Changing Woman is also called White Shell Woman, who is the main creator of the four primary clans and is considered the mother of Diné people. When a young girl transitions into a young woman, she assumes Changing Woman's authority, power, strength, and other qualities through the Kinaaldá ceremony. All in the family and community celebrate this ceremony. It acknowledges and honors family, relationships, and community. K'é and k'éí are foundational in this ceremony and the experience.

Figure 5 Diné relatives from the field.

K'é and k'éí are family. In Diné, family consists of the nuclear unit, the extended family network, clans, and relations with the earth and the universe. No distinctions exist between these units.

K'é is a daily presence for all persons. It enforces respect, kindness, cooperation, friendliness, reciprocal relations, and love. Along with k'éí, it frames the view of the universe as a web of relations. No disconnections are present. K'é is the basis for giving, sharing, and supporting relatives and clans. K'éí reinforces this by descent and clan relations. When individuals share one or more of the four clans, the group composes a shik'éí. A family connection is established, and people address each other with the proper family term, such as shimá, shizhé'é, or shimásáni. Each Diné person will have numerous relatives.

Hózhǫ describes a condition in which everything is in its proper place and functioning in harmonious relation with everything else. It is the ideal human beings strive to live by and for. This harmonious way of life is a continual thread extending in all dimensions and time. K'é and k'éí help each person strive for and achieve it in life.

FIVE
Níhi Kéyah

M ore than 300,000 people identify as Diné, and more than 150,000 people live on the reservation.[1] The current reservation land base is 27,413 square miles, larger than ten of the fifty states in the United States of America. The original reservation was created in 1868. The Navajo name for the reservation is Naabeehó Bináhásdzo. Diné Bikéyah and Naabeehó Bikéyah is Diné/Navajo land, and Dinétah refers to the ancestral homeland, often the specific location where the people emerged into this world. Níhi Kéyah is the land the people live and walk on and call home. Six major mountains bound the land. The Diyin Dine'é created Níhi Kéyah and told the people to stay within its confines because it was made specifically for them.

The land means the world to the Diné people, and this chapter discusses its philosophy, origins, history of the people's removal and return, increase in the reservation land base, challenges to the land (such as mining), and reflections on what the land means for each Diné person. While many Native nations and communities have been removed from their original land bases and live elsewhere, Diné people have continued to live on their Indigenous land base, even though some of the Indigenous land is not part of the current reservation boundaries.

Níhi Kéyah is more than a commodity and property for the Diné; it is strongly connected to their identity. Níhi Kéyah is a physical, emotional, psychological, and spiritual presence for the people. The land is part of the core of what it means to be human and Diné. The land's energy and power are reflected in the origin narratives and Diné philosophy.

Creation Narratives and Philosophy

As in chapter 1, this narrative focuses on experiences and not a chronological timeline. The version in this section of the chapter comes from a couple of sources: *Navajo History*, volume 1, edited by Ethelou Yazzie, and *Origins of the Diné*, by Mike Mitchell.[2]

In the Diné creation scripture, Áłtsé Hastiin (First Man) and Áłtsé Asdzą́ą́ (First Woman) formed the six sacred mountains with soil from the mountains gathered in the Third World. In some narratives, this takes place in the Fourth World, and in other stories, the Fifth World.

Áłtsé Hastiin and Áłtsé Asdzą́ą́ started in the east and planted the sacred mountain of the east, Sis Naajiní. They put a blanket of white shell down and sprinkled some of the soil First Man brought from the previous worlds, and more white shell was placed on top and wrapped. Yoołgai Ashkii (White Bead Boy, or Dawn Boy) was told to live in the mountain of the east. Tsoodził, mountain of the south, was planted similarly with turquoise. Dootł'izhii At'ééd (Turquoise Girl) was told to live in the mountain of the south. Dook'o'oosłííd, mountain of the west, was planted with abalone. Diichiłi Ashkii (Abalone Shell Boy) was told to live in the mountain of the west. Dibé Nitsaa, mountain of the north, was planted with obsidian. Bááshzhinii At'ééd (Obsidian Girl) was told to live in the mountain of the north.

Áłtsé Hastiin and Áłtsé Asdzą́ą́ fastened the mountains to the earth. Sis Naajiní was tied with a bolt of white lightning. They covered the mountain with a blanket of daylight and decorated it with black clouds and male rain. Shash (bear) was sent to guard the doorway for Yoołgai Ashkii.

Tsoodził was fastened with a stone knife. The mountain was covered with a blue cloud and decorated with dark mists and female rain. Tł'iish tsoh (big snake) was sent to guard the doorway for Dootł'izhii At'ééd. Dook'o'oosłííd was fastened with a sunbeam. The mountain was covered with a yellow cloud and decorated with black clouds and male rain. Niłch'í diłhił (black wind) was sent to guard the doorway for Diichiłi Ashkii.

Dibé Nitsaa was fastened with a rainbow. The mountain was covered with darkness and decorated with obsidian. Atsiniłtł'ish (lightning) was sent to guard the doorway for Bááshzhinii At'ééd.

Within these mountains, the Diyin Dine'é created the first sweat bath and hogan. They created the sun, moon, stars, and seasons. Along with these creations, the female entities realized they had become pregnant during the separation of the sexes. The separation of the sexes occurred when the male and female entities disagreed on the importance of life and who deserved credit. The female entities separated from the male entities, and they lived apart for quite some time. During this separation, female entities gave birth to monsters and placed their babies in meadows, mountains, canyons, on top of rocks, and in some cases in the middle of nowhere. The babies survived, matured, and terrorized the people. The Diyin Dine'é met to discuss how to deal with the monsters. They decided that a baby girl would be born who would help resolve this problem.

One morning Ch'óol'į'į was covered with clouds. The clouds were ádiłhxił (male black cloud), k'os diłhxił (female black cloud), niłtsą́ bika' (male rain), niłtsą́ bi'áád (female rain), and neestiin (mist). Within the clouds, a sacred area was formed, and inside this sacred space, under a rainbow, a baby girl was born. It took four days to create the baby girl. Songs, prayers, and chants were sung. Within twelve days, the baby girl became a beautiful young woman and started her menstrual cycle. She would be known as White Shell Woman, or Changing Woman.

One day Changing Woman was gathering wood before sundown. She sat down on a rock to rest for a while. The wood was tied in a bundle on her back. When she tried to pick up the bundle, something held it down. She could not stand. She struggled to lift the bundle, and after the fourth attempt, she looked up and saw a young man standing near her. The man, through powers, impregnated her. Later at a waterfall, the young man impregnated her again. She did not know who this young man was but later found out it was the Sun Bearer. In time, Changing Woman gave birth to twins. It was a difficult process. Naayéé' Neezghání (Monster Slayer) and Tó Bájísh Chíní (Child Born of Water) were born with the help of the Diyin Dine'é.

Their mother and the Diyin Dine'é loved them. They played around their home, and as they got older, they asked about their father. Changing Woman would not answer them or would say some other person is their father, trying to mislead the twins. She feared Sun Bearer would kill her sons.

One day as the twins were playing close by, the earth started to shake, and Changing Woman immediately hid her sons inside their hogan. A giant monster came and demanded to know whose tiny tracks were outside. Changing Woman was able to persuade the monster that she had made those tiny tracks. He left, and the twins came out of hiding, vowing to kill the giant. They were not afraid. They asked their mom constantly about their father. When she felt they were ready, she told them their father was the Sun Bearer. She described him as powerful and mean. They wanted to visit him to ask for his help to destroy the monsters. They said their farewells to their mother and left on their long journey to their father's house. Changing Woman wished her sons well and prayed for their safety.

The twins met several entities on their journey to see their father. Some of the entities included Na'ash jé'ii 'Asdzą́ą́ (Spider Woman), Haashch'ééshzhiní (Fire God), and Wóóshiyishí (Measuring Worm). The twins had to overcome many tests and challenges along the way. When they arrived at their father's house, they faced more challenges, overcoming each one through the use of sacred names, prayers, chants, and powers. They were able to enter the house. A beautiful entity met them and asked what they wanted. They told her they wanted to see their father, but she knew that the Sun Bearer would try to kill them when he returned. She hid them, and when the Sun Bearer returned, he asked about the two boys. The wife scolded the Sun Bearer for having children with another entity while he searched the home for them. He eventually found them and tried to kill them immediately. He tested them twice, and they remained unharmed. They were then allowed to sleep at their father's house. When they woke up, the Sun Bearer tested them again. They survived. Finally, the Sun Bearer conceded that the twins were his children.

The Sun Bearer offered the twins many gifts, but they refused and requested two weapons to help them kill the monsters. The two weapons were 'atsiniltł'ish k'aa' (zigzag lightning arrow) and 'atsoolghał k'aa' (straight lightning arrow). Sun Bearer thought about it for some time and decided to give them the weapons, even though some of the monsters were his children. He requested that when they killed Yé'iitsoh T'áálá'í Naagháii, they bring him the headdress. They agreed. The Sun Bearer gave Monster Slayer a zigzag lightning arrow and Child Born of Water a straight lightning arrow. He told them information about Yé'iitsoh, too.

The twins traveled to Tó Sido (Hot Springs) near Mount Taylor via lightning bolt. They waited for Yé'iitsoh, who returned to the lake, where they confronted him. Two powerful lightning flashes hit Yé'iitsoh, killing him. They also prevented his blood from coming back together and reaching the lake. If it had, he would have been brought back to life. The twins acquired the headdress and gave it to their father as he requested. They cut up Yé'iitsoh's body and placed the parts in different locations around Níhi Kéyah. They also scalped him and took the scalp home with them. They returned home and told their mother about their adventures, meeting their father, and killing Yé'iitsoh. Changing Woman did not believe her sons until they showed her Yé'iitsoh's scalp.

Monster Slayer went out to kill the other monsters on his own, and his brother watched him via two wands, k'eet'áán yáłti'. One was a medicine wand and the other a prayer wand. If Monster Slayer needed help, the wands would start to burn brightly. Child Born of Water smoked the medicine wand and blew it on the prayer wand in the four directions and prayed for his brother. This was supposed to give Monster Slayer renewed strength to destroy the monsters.

Monster Slayer searched for the monsters all over the land, and he was able to track down many and kill them. He returned home, and in a short time, he saw red smoke way off in the distance. He went to investigate and found a hole in the ground. In the hole, he saw old men. He learned that these old men were sleep, hunger, poverty, lice, and old age. He wanted to kill them all, but they were able to persuade him not to kill them because the people would suffer without them. He traveled to all corners of Níhi Kéyah to make sure all the monsters were dead. When no other monsters were located, he returned home, where he informed his mother and brother of what he had found.

The twins' work was finished. They laid down their weapons and took off their armor, returning everything to their father, who in return provided them gifts. The twins wanted all the gifts their father showed them. He agreed to their request. The people obtained wild animals, domesticated animals, fruits, vegetables, precious stones, rain, wind, snow, and many other things.

They returned to their mother and settled down near her home. After a short period, Monster Slayer had nightmares and disappeared for days searching for monsters. He saw monsters everywhere he went, and Changing Woman was concerned for her son. The Diyin Dine'é gathered to discuss his condition, and one of them said the spirits of the slain monsters had come back to torment his conscience. A ceremony was created to address the issue, and elements of the Enemy Way ceremony (Nidáá') comes from this creation. The ceremony worked on the fourth try, and Monster Slayer lived a healthy life.

The Sun Bearer asked Changing Woman to live with him. He promised to build a beautiful home on an island in the ocean to the west, where everything would be provided for her. She did not want to leave

Níhi Kéyah, but her sons, Diyin Dine'é, and Sun Bearer convinced her to move to her new home in the west. Her sons also went with her. Soon Diyin Dine'é met to discuss who would live at Níhi Kéyah. Changing Woman heard the news and thought humans should inhabit the land. She created humans by rubbing skin from her breast, back, and under both arms. From these first humans, she created the first four clans. The skin from her breast formed the Kinyaa'áanii (Towering House); the skin from her back formed the Honágháahnii (One Who Walks Around You); the skin from her right armpit formed the Tódích'íi'nii (Bitter Water); and the skin from her left armpit formed the Hashtł'ishnii (Mud). She gave each group a cane of white shell, turquoise, abalone, and jet as well as an animal protector of bear, mountain lion, bull snake, and porcupine. Each group was given water, roasted corn, meat jerky, and corn pollen.

With the animal protectors, the four groups left for Níhi Kéyah. They encountered different entities and peoples along their journey. The animal protectors fought off enemies. The people used their canes to find water at various locations. They walked a long distance and came through various points before reaching a place between Ch'óol'į'į (Gobernador Knob in New Mexico) and Dził Ná'ooditii (Huerfano Mountain in New Mexico). The place is Dinétah (Place of the People) because it is where Changing Woman lived and raised her children. First Man and First Woman also lived in the area. The Diné people were home.

The Diyin Dine'é became very close to the people and visited numerous times. They taught them hunting and weaving. Through these teachings, the people lived and settled within the six sacred mountains.

Bosque Redondo/Reservation

Beginning in the sixteenth and continuing into the nineteenth century, Spanish and Mexican ways influenced the Diné peoples. A significant influence was the introduction of livestock—sheep, goats, cows, and horses. It is important to note, according to the creation scripture, that the Sun Bearer introduced sheep to the people when his sons, the twin protectors, brought sheep back to the people.

Besides taking care of the sheep and learning how to use the horse effectively, warfare affected the people. Spanish, Mexican, New Mexican, and American military conflicts occurred from 1540 to 1868. The Navajo people defended themselves against the Spanish, Mexicans, New Mexicans, Americans, Comanches, and Utes. The conflicts resulted in the capture or death of Diné men, women, and children. Conflicts with the Spanish and the Mexicans usually were attempts by family members or relatives to rescue loved ones.

The people adapted to the changing situations to ensure their survival. They worked together and moved around the land. They helped one another secure the safest homes. More changes took place with the American invasion and the people's internment at Bosque Redondo.

From 1846 to 1864, conflicts between the American military and the people were frequent. Several treaties were signed to make peace, but all were broken. New Mexicans wanted the federal government to protect them from the Diné people, but for the most part, the people kept to themselves and did not raid Pueblo and New Mexican settlements, although some Diné individuals did so.

In the summer of 1863, U.S. Army general James Carleton ordered Colonel Christopher "Kit" Carson to attack and punish the Diné people. Carson employed Utes, various Pueblos, Hopis, and the Diné Anaa'i to help in his campaign. By the winter of 1863–64, thousands of Diné people had surrendered to Carson. Carson effectively carried out a scorched earth policy to subdue and subjugate the people. From 1864 to 1866, Carson and the U.S. military rounded up thousands of Diné men, women, and children and forced them to march over three hundred miles to the Bosque Redondo prison camp in eastern New Mexico, near present-day Fort Sumner. From 1864 to 1866, ten thousand Diné people marched and lived at the Bosque Redondo prison camp. While thousands were at Fort Sumner, hundreds eluded capture and hid in the Grand Canyon, in the Navajo Mountain region, or among various Pueblo villages with relatives. They maintained cultural aspects while remaining watchful for the possibility of a U.S. attack.

The Diné people suffered tremendously at Bosque Redondo. The people know Bosque Redondo as Hwéeldi, which means "people suffering." The land at Bosque Redondo could not sustain corn because nearby Pecos River was salty. The people depended on government food rations, but the food was so different, it made them weak and sick, with some people dying from it. In addition, the Comanches, Kiowas, Mexicans, and New Mexicans raided the camp and stole women and children to sell as slaves. Diseases ravaged the camp, and many people died during the incarceration.[3] Even with the enormous suffering, the medicine people prayed to keep everyone strong and hopeful. They wanted desperately to return to Níhi Kéyah.

The Diné leadership at the time did not want their families to suffer anymore and constantly begged the U.S. military to allow them to return home. Barboncito, Manuelito, Armijo, Delgadito, Herrero, Torivio, and Largo negotiated with the U.S. government to return home.

In the spring of 1868, because of the enormous costs and the obvious failure of Bosque Redondo in government officials' eyes, the federal government sent General William T. Sherman and Colonel Samuel F. Tappan to rectify the situation and to negotiate a treaty with the people. A treaty was signed on June 1, 1868, allowing the people to return to Níhi Kéyah. The treaty stipulated that the people would no longer "raid," and that they must stay within the reservation boundaries established by the federal government.[4] The reservation boundaries were the following:

Bounded on the north by the 37th degree of north latitude, south by an east and west line passing through the site of old Fort Defiance, in Canon Bonito, east by the parallel of longitude which, if prolonged south, would pass through old Fort Lyon, or the Ojo-de-oso, Bear Spring, and west by the parallel of longitude about 109'30' west of Greenwich, provided it embraces the outlet of the Canon-de-Chilly [*sic*], which canon is to be all included in this reservation, shall be, and the same is hereby, set apart for the use and occupation of the Navajo tribe of Indians, and for such other friendly tribes or individual Indians as from time to time they may be willing, with the consent of the United States, to admit among them; and the United States agrees that no persons except those herein so authorized to do.[5]

The treaty also stipulated that the people could not oppose the building of railroad lines through their homeland, and they were required to send their children to government schools. The federal government in return would provide seeds, farm equipment, and livestock.

The people left Fort Sumner on June 18, 1868. More than 7,300 people walked the thirty-five days to reach Fort Wingate, New Mexico. They stayed at Fort Wingate until January 1869. Livestock was not distributed until November 1869. Each man, woman, and child received two animals. Barboncito, one of the leaders who signed the treaty, spoke of the importance of this livestock: "Now you are beginning again. Take care of the sheep that have been given to you, as you care for your own children. Never kill them for food. If you are hungry, go out after the wild animals and the wild plants. Or go without food, for you have done that before. These few sheep must grow into flocks so that we, the people, can be as we once were."[6]

The impact of Hwéeldi was traumatic and life altering. The people began to see themselves as one nation; new traditions developed; men learned new trades; women used commercial yarn for weaving; and the people were exposed to American and Christian thought, ways, values, and attitudes. Níhi Kéyah helped the people grow and prosper for the next sixty-plus years, from 1868 to the 1930s.

The people returned to where they had been living prior to Hwéeldi. No signposts or fences existed, and the government did not force the people to live within the stated reservation boundaries. Within ten years, President Rutherford B. Hayes signed an executive order pushing the reservation boundary twenty miles to the west because the Diné people had lobbied the federal government to increase the reservation boundaries. For the next sixty years, lands were added to the reservation via executive orders and congressional confirmation. Most of the additional lands were on the western part of the reservation in Arizona territory. Allotments and opposition from the New Mexico congressional delegation fenced in the eastern part of the reservation. The eastern part of the reservation developed into a patchwork of reservation and nonreservation land, known as the checkerboard area.

Challenges

The people went through a huge transition from the end of World War II in 1945 through the 1980s. Education, health care, economic development, voting rights, religious freedom, mineral extraction, and the changing economy transformed the people and way of life. More people began to work in the wage labor system, and children were sent to boarding schools created to educate Diné youth away from their families and communities. Western education became the foremost priority for the people, but the repercussions of boarding schools, special vocational programs, and public and parochial schools were traumatic and life altering. Diné bizaad was prohibited, and many families encouraged their children to learn to speak English. Along with Western education, more people left the reservation to get away from the problems of the reservation and the "backwards" way of life.

The Navajo Tribal Council sought ways to develop the reservation economy, including allowing mining companies onto Níhi Kéyah. In many cases, council decisions were done for the betterment of communities, but the results negatively affected the people. For example, Kerr-McGee and Vanadium Corporation of America established uranium mines on the reservation in the 1950s.[7] The companies never told the people or the council the dangers of working in uranium mines.

From 1952 to 1963, hundreds of Diné men worked for Kerr-McGee in the uranium mines near Shiprock, New Mexico. Hundreds died later from lung cancer.[8] Other mineral extraction projects were approved by the council in the 1960s, such as Peabody Coal Company mining on Black Mesa. The approval of Peabody Coal Company to mine Black Mesa and to use precious underground water to transport the coal to the Mohave generating power plant in Nevada, lead to the removal of hundreds of Diné families from their homes and some Hopi families from the 1970s to the 2000s.

Along with mineral extraction development challenges on Níhi Kéyah, overgrazing was a concern. The federal government took the approach that the Diné people needed to reduce their livestock, which the people strongly opposed. The people were never consulted about how to handle overgrazing. The federal government implemented live-stock reduction in the 1930s and continued into the 1940s. Many families lost their self-sufficiency, and many left the reservation to find work in border towns and cities such as Phoenix and Albuquerque.

Industrial development on the land became a central fixture for the Navajo economy in the late 1940s and 1950s. It did provide some positive aspects along with negative consequences to the land and to the people, such as lack of sanitation, water, utilities, and housing. Tourism became more prominent, especially when Hollywood director John Ford filmed seven movies in Monument Valley from 1939 to 1960. The John Ford films created international interest in the Diné people, bringing thousands of tourists who wanted to see John Wayne and Native peoples. It also helped create some infrastructure, such as paved roads and the first Navajo tribal park at Monument Valley in 1960.

Large parcels of lands were added to the original reservation because of the people living far apart from one another, the high number of live-stock grazing the lands, and the efforts of effective Diné leaders such as Henry "Chee" Dodge lobbying Congress, not an easy task. In the late 1800s and early 1900s, presidents Rutherford B. Hayes, Chester A. Arthur, Grover Cleveland, William McKinley, Theodore Roosevelt,

Woodrow Wilson, Herbert Hoover, and Franklin D. Roosevelt through executive orders added lands to the original Navajo reservation. Congress put a stop to this when they passed a law proposed by Arizona representative Marcus Aurelius Smith, who opposed providing more land to the Navajo Nation in the state of Arizona. From this point forward, the Navajo Nation needed to protect what they had and be on guard for the possibility of losing land. The Diné people would also be required to put more effort into lobbying the government for additional lands for the reservation. A good portion of the eastern part of the reservation in New Mexico was allotted and acquiring more land was stopped through the efforts of the New Mexico congressional delegation and a few Diné leaders, such as Jacob Morgan.[9] Morgan did not want more grazing lands added because he wanted the people to acculturate to a Western way of living, where sheep herding and ranching was in the past. Additional lands in Arizona and southeastern Utah were designated as part of the Navajo reservation during this time.

With these constant challenges, the people, council delegates, and allies worked hard to ensure Níhi Kéyah was protected from outside intervention and oppression. In the twenty-first century, the Diné people are still confronted with many challenges, including environmental protection, economic development, education, health care, public safety, and other pertinent issues. The land remains significant and sacred for the people, as reflected in the following perspectives.

Reflections

These reflections represent only a fraction of what the land means to each Diné person. Numerous perspectives about the land are evident. Some will be similar, others distinct, yet the overall theme is that the land is beautiful, significant to the people, and will always be home for each person, community, and the entire nation.

These personal perspectives come from the written words of Luci Tapahonso, Laura Tohe, Irvin Morris, Mae Tso, Roberta Blackgoat, Pauline Whitesinger, and Ruth Benally. Conversations about the land and what it means to each Diné person come from the heart. Some of the simplest questions to ask are, What does the land mean to you? and, What comes to mind when you think of Níhi Kéyah?

Luci Tapahonso's poems and words describe the people's history of the land. Her stories about Shiprock, the people, and the reservation show strength and understanding of the land. In her poetry piece "The Holy People Lived Here" in *A Radiant Curve*, she writes: "The Holy People lived here in the beginning. They built the first hooghan, made the first weapons, sang the first songs, and made the first prayers. Diné language, ceremonies, history, and beliefs began here. This is where we began."[10]

She shows the existential connection the people have to Níhi Kéyah and that this connection cannot be severed or taken away.

Laura Tohe, also through poetry, shows how she views, feels, and connects to the earth. In *Tséyi' Deep in the Rock: Reflections on Canyon De Chelly*, she writes in her poem "Dinétah": "The silver breath of a thousand horses, and it is only yours that I seek. I happily step over into existence, into our canyons, our rivers, our mountains, our valleys. Sky beauty above and earth beauty below. Oh, how I've missed you. To think I was away for so long, and you were always there, waiting on the red earth to hold yourself open and offer to carry my burden."[11] For each Diné person, the land is home, and home is the land.

Irvin Morris, in *From the Glittering World: A Navajo Story*, writes in "Shikéyah (My homeland)": "From my house, on a clear morning—because we are situated high up on the alluvial apron fronting the Chuska Mountains—I can see a wide sweep of my beloved homeland. From there, I am reminded of who I am: I am not alone, nor am I the first. The land has birthed and sustained all my grandmothers and grandfathers. Áhál">áanee'."[12]

Níhi Kéyah is home, and home has to be respected and honored. It has a long history, and the Diné people living and walking on it understand it well. The federal government and many non-Diné do not necessarily view the land similarly, and in many cases disrespect and dishonor Níhi Kéyah.

Malcolm Benally's *Bitter Water: Diné Oral Histories of the Navajo-Hopi Land Dispute* highlights four Diné women who resisted removal from their home and worked hard to carry on a Diné way of life in a world where encroaching Western values, ideologies, and ways had fractured the people and the land. Mae Tso talks about her continuing fight to stay on her homeland and not relocate. She says, "We have become this land of ours. . . . I have my own prayers and songs. Why should I give this up and walk away?"[13]

Roberta Blackgoat talks about the people's placement on the land. She says, "When the people were placed we became the Navajo Nation. The creator placed our roots here. 'Take care of the land. If this is the way you *live*, the land will nourish you,' is a teaching that begins the moment you're born here on the land."[14] She discusses the importance of taking care of the land and carrying on the prayers and offerings.

Pauline Whitesinger describes the relocation's impact on the people and the land. She says, "All the chaos in life comes into our homes now. 'You'll be relocated. If you resist you will be beaten.' This is what we are told. Why do they want to beat us? Why do they want to use the relocation law against me?"[15] She recognizes the land as a mother and the protection she provides. The land and the nourishment it provides all life is the basis for the respect Whitesinger, Blackgoat, Tso, and many Diné people have for Níhi Kéyah.

Ruth Benally stresses the importance of life and how the land is an integral system. She says, "Life is at the cornfield; the cornfield is how we have survived. It is how we live here."[16] Without the land, there is no life. For the people, the land is interwoven with each living being. Ruth respects this system, and she wants to protect and maintain Níhi Kéyah.

Figure 6 Family home area of the author's mother in Naschitti, New Mexico.

Each Diné person mentioned has a deep love and connection to the land and what it means. The land means support, love, and deep spiritual connections, and it grounds the people to the earth and universe.

Conclusion

Níhi Kéyah is home. It is a sacred place for the Diné people. The Diyin Dine'é created this land and instructed the people to live within its confines because it was specifically made to always protect them. Diné identity is the land. More than three hundred thousand Diné people are connected to Níhi Kéyah, and more than half of them live on the reservation, while many others live close in neighboring cities and towns.

The land is the world for the Diné people, and this chapter has discussed its philosophy, origins, history of the people's removal and return, annexation of lands, challenges, and individual reflections. The chapter has shown how the land is integral to the people's identity. The people worked hard to sustain their original land base, even though some of the original land is no longer part of the current reservation.

Níhi Kéyah is more than property or a commodity to the Diné people. It is their existence, world, and who they are as Diné. The land is a physical, emotional, psychological, and spiritual presence for the people. The land is strongly connected to the people's humanity and what it means to live. The land has energy and power that provides the necessary support and love for the Diné people, as it does for human beings in all places.

Conclusion

iné identity remains strong, though challenges have arisen and will continue to do so in the coming generations. The Navajo Nation has a strong enrollment of more than three hundred thousand citizens, many of whom have adapted aspects of American customs, values, and beliefs—yet Diné identity continues. SNBH, Diné bizaad, k'é, k'éí, Níhi Kéyah, and Diné baa hane' construct Diné identity. These markers offer a glimpse into a diverse and distinct group. Diné people are creating and sustaining an identity conducive to the twenty-first century. This book was not designed to declare the "true and authentic" Diné person but rather to offer perspectives.

Diné people are proud to be Diné, although many Diné people do not know their history, way of life, and/or the language. They do not know their clans or their clans' histories. Many have limited Diné cultural knowledge. For some, the only exposure to Diné cultural knowledge is when they visit grandparents, other relatives, and friends who live and speak only in Diné. They may not see themselves as Diné or live a Diné way of life. One way to change this is to educate people about their history, way of life, and language. It is a challenge for institutions like

Diné College, Navajo Technical University, and regional universities such as Northern Arizona University, Arizona State University, University of Arizona, Fort Lewis College, and the University of New Mexico to focus exclusively on Diné histories and languages. The question is how much more or what else can be done to maintain and sustain Diné bizaad and Diné baa hane'.

Navajo enrollment is fairly strict, with individuals needing to possess one-quarter or more Navajo blood and to be a descendant of a person who is on the 1940 census tribal roll. With this strict requirement, the Navajo Nation has blossomed, although many more could enroll who do not meet the one-quarter requirement.

Navajo history shows that the people have always had intertribal relations and marriages with other communities, such as Zunis, Hopis, Apaches, Utes, Jemez, and other Native peoples. Navajos have over sixty clans, including Naasht'ézhi Dine'é (Zuni clan), Ma'iideeshgiizhnii (Jemez clan), Naakaii Dine'é (Mexican clan), Nooda'i Dine'é (Ute clan), and Naashgali Dine'é (Mescalero Apache clan). The current enrollment criteria will need to be scrutinized to develop an alternative criteria that is inclusive and not exclusive of Diné blood and racial groups.

Diné scholar Yolynda Begay's "Historic and Demographic Changes that Impact the Future of the Diné and the Development of Community-Based Policy," in *Diné Perspectives: Revitalizing and Reclaiming Navajo Thought*, analyzed present-day and historical Navajo population dynamics and how these dynamics affect enrollment policy. From 1990 to 2003, the thirteen-year average of intertribal and interracial relationships for Diné men and women was 49.1 percent.[1] This number has probably risen over 50 percent since 2003. The data indicates that at the current rate, the Navajo Nation continues to differ racially and demographically from the time when great-grandparents and grandparents were children. Other pertinent statistics indicate that the total population within the Navajo reservation boundaries declined by over 6 percent from 2000 to 2010, and that there was an increase in the number of Diné mixed heritage citizens from the 1930s to the 2000s.

The data show that Navajo enrollment criteria changes are warranted. According to Begay, approximately 38 percent of the newborn Navajo population is full blood.

While there are many questions to answer on Diné identity and enrollment, Diné identity is constantly changing because of each Diné person and community. Diné thought, language, relations, clans, history, and the land reflect these changes. These changes are persistent.

This book nonetheless has several implications for Diné identity, enrollment, and Navajo Nation building. First, Diné identity is dynamic and fluid. As history has shown, Diné peoples and communities have had to adjust to many challenges, from relocation to livestock reduction to uranium mining to oppression, yet they have always sustained their identity. This fluidity illustrates how Diné peoples can confront changes and the pressures of living in a twenty-first century world and beyond.

Second, Diné men and women have different perspectives on identity, and all of these views represent a "true and authentic way" to be Diné. These perspectives will be similar and distinct and cannot be dismissed because they represent who the people are in the twenty-first century. Diné people comprise many different clans, locations, ways, and experiences.

Third, Diné identity is distinctive from any other American Indian peoples and communities. While many, if not all, Native peoples and communities might have similar histories and experiences, they are not the same. What Diné people have experienced makes their identity distinctive and reflective of what it means to be Diné and not any other Native group. So, this indicates future enrollment criteria will need to include and reflect what is Diné and how the people live and relate to one another.

Fourth, Navajo enrollment should be changed to reflect the changing nature of the people. Diné people have always adapted to their environment. This adaptation does not make Diné identity and way of life unoriginal but rather shows a vibrant group. What Navajo enrollment should be in the future is the people's determination.

Fifth, Diné identity should be seen as open-ended rather than defined by a litmus test of characteristics, such as a Diné person being Diné only if they speak the language, grew up on the reservation, know how to herd sheep, or wear turquoise jewelry. This type of representation reflects only one aspect of Diné identity, when there are many cultural aspects to being Diné. Many Diné people do not speak Diné; while Diné bizaad continuance is important, it should not be a barrier to exclude Diné people who do not speak it. This brings only disharmony and resentment. While an open-ended approach might be healthier, it does create a dilemma for the people. The dilemma is that language both does and does not establish Diné identity, because language maintenance and revitalization is a challenge for the people. The willingness to have a flexible perspective on Diné identity offers an effective way to live; inflexibility can deteriorate Navajo communities.

Sixth, Diné identity should not be viewed as a controversial or divisive subject in Navajo communities and families. It should be discussed and understood by everyone. Everyone should be given the opportunity to participate in such discussion. While identity markers represent Diné identity now and into the future, Diné people should also realize adaptation, flexibility, and human connection are a part of what it means to be Diné. Throughout Navajo history, the people have always included others as part of their families and communities. This continues.

In this book, I wanted to discuss and examine Diné identity markers. The people are sustaining these markers. Each person lives an independent and distinct life, at the same time maintaining connection to the Navajo Nation. These markers are the foundation of Diné peoples and communities. Euro-American colonialism and imperialism has influenced how the people think and act, but the people maintain and sustain what it means to be Diné. Diné identity is strong, confident, and positive, and each Diné person represents this now and in the future.

Prosperity and wellness for all Diné people is the goal. Diné people are like no other people in the world. This distinctiveness has been

Figure 7 We are still here.

ongoing for over a millennia, and the people will ensure its viability. The Diné people call themselves Diné (People), Nihokáá Dine'é (Earth Surface People), Bíla'ashla'ii Dine'é (Five-Fingered Human Beings), and the Diyin Nohookáá Dine'é (Holy Earth Surface People). Each of these names is who the Diné people were, are, and will be. This is present and true.

NOTES

Introduction

1. Charlotte Frisbie, *Kinaaldá: A Study of the Navaho Girl's Puberty Ceremony* (Middletown, Conn.: Wesleyan University Press, 1967).

2. Ruth Roessel, *Women in Navajo Society* (Rough Rock, Ariz.: Navajo Resource Center, 1981).

3. Roessel, *Women in Navajo Society.*

4. Charlotte Goodluck, "Understanding Navajo Ethnic Identity: Weaving the Meaning through the Voices of Young Girls" (PhD diss., University of Denver, 1998).

5. Amy J. Schulz, "Navajo Women and the Politics of Identity," *Social Problems* 45 (1998): 3, 336–55.

6. Miranda J. Haskie, "Preserving a Culture: Practicing the Navajo Principles of Hózhó dóó K'é" (PhD diss., Fielding Graduate Institute, 2002).

7. Clyde Kluckhohn, "The Philosophy of Navaho Indians," in *Readings in Anthropology*, vol. 2 (New York: Crowell, 1959), 424–49.

8. Kluckhohn, "Philosophy of Navaho Indians," 424–49.

9. John Farella, *The Main Stalk: A Synthesis of Navajo Philosophy* (Albuquerque: University of New Mexico Press, 1984).

10. Wilson Aronilth Jr., *Foundation of Culture* (Tsaile, Ariz.: Diné College, 1992).

11. Kristina Jacobsen, *The Sound of Navajo Country: Music, Language, and Diné Belonging* (Chapel Hill: University of North Carolina Press, 2017).

12. Lloyd L. Lee, *Diné Masculinities: Conceptualizations and Reflections* (North Charleston, S.C.: CreateSpace, 2013).

13. Jack D. Forbes, "Blood Quantum: A Relic of Racism and Termination," the People's Voice, the Weyanoke Association, November 27, 2000, http://weyanoke.org/reading/jdf-BloodQuantum.html.

14. Bill Donovan, "Census: Navajo Enrollment tops 300,000," *Navajo Times*, July 7, 2011, final edition.

15. The U.S. Census Bureau issued an overview brief in January 2012 detailing the American Indian and Alaska Native population. The charts and statistics reveal how many individuals identify as Navajo. U.S. Census Bureau, *The American Indian and Alaska Native Population: 2010.* Washington, D.C.: Department of Commerce, Economics and Statistics Administration, Census Bureau, 2012.

16. Peter Iverson, *Diné: A History of the Navajos* (Albuquerque: University of New Mexico Press, 2002).

17. Martha Austin and Regina Lynch, eds., *Saad Ahaah Sinil Dual Language: A Navajo-English Dictionary*, rev. ed. (Chinle, Ariz.: Rough Rock Press, 1990).

18. Paul Spruhan, "The Origins, Current Status, and Future Prospects of Blood Quantum as the Definition of Membership in the Navajo Nation," *Tribal Law Journal* 8, no. 1 (2007): 1–17.

19. The separate resolution was Navajo Nation Council Resolution CJ-50-53, July 1953.

20. Resolution CJ-50-53, 7.

21. The following newspapers documented the call for revising the blood quantum limit and the subsequent discussions following the idea: the *Gallup Independent*, the *Farmington Daily Times*, the *Arizona Republic*, and the *Salt Lake Tribune*. Some of the discussion might be archived at the indianz.com website.

Chapter 1

1. Ethelou Yazzie, ed., *Navajo History*, vol. 1 (Rough Rock, Ariz.: Navajo Curriculum Center, 1971).

2. Entities do reflect human thought and behavior.

3. Iverson, *Diné*, 8–16.

4. Iverson, *Diné*, 8–16.

5. From this point on, the terms humans, human beings, people, Diné, and Navajo refer to the five-fingered people inhabiting the Fifth World and the earth.

6. In Navajo communities, the self, family, community, culture, nation, and universe are equally divided between male and female. One cannot be without the other, and both balance life.

7. McAllester, *Hogans*.

8. Some scholars view this era as a period when Navajo culture was developing in Dinétah. They also bring in known archaeological evidence to point to a distinct Navajo culture. One theory proposes that Navajo people originated from the Anasazi. Some Navajo healers believe this, while others do not.

9. Iverson, *Diné*.

10. Lynn Robinson Bailey, *Indian Slave Trade in the Southwest: A Study of Slave-Taking and the Traffic in Indian Captives* (Los Angeles, Calif.: Westernlore Press, 1966); Frank McNitt, *Navajo Wars: Military Campaigns, Slave Raids, and Reprisals* (Albuquerque: University of New Mexico Press, 1972); Iverson, *Diné*; David M. Brugge, *Navajos in the Catholic Church Records of New Mexico, 1694–1875* (Tsaile, Ariz.: Navajo Community College Press, 1985).

11. Iverson, *Diné*, 28.

12. Iverson, *Diné*, 29.

13. The people at Tóhajiileehé are a part of the Navajo Nation. Generally speaking, most Navajos do not view them as less Navajo or non-Navajo.

14. Iverson, *Diné*, 47.

15. "Peaceable inhabitants" were mostly Anglo ranchers and Hispano farmers.

16. Iverson, *Diné*, 47.

17. Carleton and others viewed the "Navajo problem" as a menace to progress and civilization. Navajo people were viewed as savages that needed to be dealt with in a savage-like way.

18. The Navajo people were forced to become Western-style farmers. The government demanded they forget about sheep raising and the Navajo way of life. The government wanted them to be Western educated and to live apart from the rest of American society.

19. Iverson, *Diné*. The business council was viewed as a rubber-stamp entity with no legitimate power to protect the best interests of the Navajo people in the 1920s. The Navajo people rejected the Indian Reorganization Act (IRA) in 1934 by commissioner of Indian affairs John Collier, but this business council developed into a tribal council not all different from most IRA tribal governments.

20. Karen D. Harvey and Lisa D. Harjo, *Indian Country: A History of Native People in America* (Golden, Colo.: North American Press, 1994).

21. Iverson, *Diné*.

22. Ruth Roessel and Broderick H. Johnson, *Navajo Livestock Reduction: A National Disgrace* (Chinle, Ariz.: Navajo Community College Press, 1974), 22.

23. These men are known as the Navajo Code Talkers. Nearly four hundred Navajo men were trained to become radiomen who would help send and receive orders using the Navajo language. There is a Navajo Code Talkers Association with fewer than five living members.

24. Iverson, *Diné*.

25. Steve Pavlik, "Navajo Christianity: Historical Origins and Modern Trends," *Wicazo Sa Review* 12, no. 2 (Fall 1997): 43–58.

26. Iverson, *Diné*.

27. Navajo Community College is now Diné College. The main campus is located in Tsaile, Arizona, with several branches located around the reservation. The school is a nationally recognized tribal college.

28. Iverson, *Diné*.

29. Donovan, "Census."

Chapter 2

1. Haskie, "Preserving a Culture," 33.

2. Haskie "Preserving a Culture," 31.

3. Haskie "Preserving a Culture," 31. The term *traditional* refers to an era in Navajo history before European invasion. It does not refer to a specific time period.

4. Haskie "Preserving a Culture," 32.

5. Aronilth, *Foundation of Culture*, 13.

6. Haskie "Preserving a Culture," 32.

7. Farella, *Main Stalk*, 153.

8. Deborah House, *Language Shift Among the Navajos: Identity Politics and Cultural Continuity* (Tucson: University of Arizona Press, 2002), 27.

9. U.S. Census Bureau, *American Indian and Alaska Native Population*.

10. Herbert John Benally, "Navajo Philosophy of Learning and Pedagogy," *Journal of Navajo Education* 12, no. 1 (Fall 1994): 24.

11. Rex Lee Jim, "A Moment in My Life," in *Here First: Autobiographical Essays by Native American Writers*, ed. Arnold Krupat and Brian Swann (New York: Modern Library, 2000), 245.

12. Jim, "A Moment in My Life," 232.

13. Jim, "A Moment in My Life," 232.

14. Jim, "A Moment in My Life," 233.

15. Jim, "A Moment in My Life," 235.

16. Jim, "A Moment in My Life," 235.

17. Lloyd L. Lee, "21st Century Diné Cultural Identity: Defining and Practicing Sa'ah Naaghai Bik'eh Hozhoon" (PhD diss., University of New Mexico, 2004), 125.

18. L. Lee, "21st Century Diné Cultural Identity," 125.

19. L. Lee, "21st Century Diné Cultural Identity," 126.

20. L. Lee, "21st Century Diné Cultural Identity," 132.

21. L. Lee, "21st Century Diné Cultural Identity," 132.

22. The two-world paradigm is used to describe contemporary Indigenous peoples in the United States. The phrase *two worlds* began to be part of everyday language descriptions of Indigenous peoples' challenges and problems in the early twentieth century. Numerous texts discuss the two-world paradigm and the traumatic effects on Indigenous peoples. Several Indigenous scholars have problems with the two-world paradigm. I also have problems with it. I believe one world exists, but a person can switch notions of their identity in multiple communities. The consequences of switching one's personal identity can have harmful affects on a human being's mental, psychological, physical, and spiritual well-being.

23. L. Lee, "21st Century Diné Cultural Identity," 133.

24. L. Lee, "21st Century Diné Cultural Identity," 134.

25. L. Lee, "21st Century Diné Cultural Identity," 135.

Chapter 3

1. U.S. Census Bureau, *American Indian and Alaska Native Population.*

2. Gary Witherspoon, *Language and Art in the Navajo Universe* (Ann Arbor: University of Michigan Press, 1977), 15–16; Mary C. Wheelwright, *Navajo Creation Myth* (Santa Fe, N.Mex.: Museum of Navajo Ceremonial Art, 1942); Leland Wyman, *Blessingway* (Tucson: University of Arizona Press, 1970).

3. Witherspoon, *Language and Art,* 16.

4. Wyman, *Blessingway,* 113–14; Witherspoon, *Language and Art,* 16.

5. Wyman, *Blessingway,* 398. The information is from Navajo hataałii Frank Mitchell. He was recorded and translated by Father Berard Haile.

6. Witherspoon, *Language and Art,* 25.

7. Witherspoon, *Language and Art*, 26–27.

8. Witherspoon, *Language and Art*, 33; Pliny Earle Goddard, "Navajo Texts," *Anthropological Papers of the American Museum of Natural History* 34 (1933): 1–179.

9. Witherspoon, *Language and Art*, 46.

10. Robert S. McPherson, *Dinéjí Na'nitin: Navajo Traditional Teachings and History* (Boulder: University Press of Colorado, 2012), 214–15.

11. McPherson, *Dinéjí Na'nitin*, 215.

12. Witherspoon, *Language and Art*, 59; Berard Haile, "Soul Concepts of the Navaho," *Annali Lateranensi* 7 (1943): 59–94.

13. Wayne Holm and Agnes Holm, "Navajo Language Education: Retrospect and Prospects," *Bilingual Research Journal* 19, no. 1 (1990): 141–67; Paul Platero, *Navajo Head Start Language Study* (Window Rock, Navajo Nation: Division of Dine Education, 1992); Evangeline Parsons-Yazzie, "Perceptions of Selected Navajo Elders Regarding Navajo Language Attrition," *Journal of Navajo Education* 12, no. 2 (1996): 51–57; Tiffany S. Lee, "If They Want Navajo to Be Learned, Then They Should Require It in All Schools: Navajo Teenagers' Experiences, Choices, and Demands Regarding Navajo Language," *Wicazo Sa Review* 22, no. 1 (Spring 2007): 7–33; Teresa L. McCarty, Mary Eunice Romero-Little, and Ofelia Zepeda, "Native American Youth Discourses on Language Shift and Retention: Ideological Cross-Currents and Their Implications for Language Planning," *International Journal of Bilingual Education and Bilingualism* 9, no. 5 (2006): 659–77; House, *Language Shift*; Joshua Fishman, *Reversing Language Shift* (Clevedon: Multilingual Matters, 1991); James Crawford, "Endangered Native American Languages: What Is to Be Done, and Why?," *Bilingual Research Journal* 19, no. 1 (Winter 1995): 17–38.

14. Tom Kee, interview by author, Albuquerque, NM, October 8, 2002.

15. Kee interview

16. Steve Thomas, interview by author, Albuquerque, NM, October 18, 2002.

17. Thomas interview.

18. Thomas interview.

19. Navajo Election Administration, accessed September 14, 2019, http://www.navajoelections.navajo-nsn.gov/index.html.

Chapter 4

1. Raymond D. Austin, *Navajo Courts and Navajo Common Law: A Tradition of Tribal Self-Governance* (Minneapolis: University of Minnesota Press, 2009), 84.

2. Lori Arviso Alvord and Elizabeth Cohen Van Pelt, *The Scalpel and the Silver Bear: The First Navajo Woman Surgeon Combines Western Medicine and Traditional Healing* (New York: Bantam Books, 1999), 8. Lori is mixed. Her mother is non-Navajo.

3. Austin, *Navajo Courts*, 137.

4. Austin, *Navajo Courts*, 139–40.

5. Austin, *Navajo Courts*, 141.

6. Austin, *Navajo Courts*, 142.

7. Diné fundamental law was codified into Title 1 of the Navajo Nation Code. The Navajo Nation Council uses the fundamental law to help govern, and the Navajo Supreme Court uses it to analyze legal cases. The fundamental law is rooted in cultural values, traditions, and ancestral knowledge. The basis of the law is traditional, customary, natural, and common. Please read Austin, *Navajo Courts*; and Lloyd L. Lee, ed., *Navajo Sovereignty: Understandings and Visions of the Diné People* (Tucson: University of Arizona Press, 2017).

8. 9 NNC § 2(b) (2005).

9. 9 NNC §§5(d) and (e) (2005).

10. Carol Shorty, interview by author, tape recording, Albuquerque, NM, October 22, 2002.

11. Shorty interview.

12. Shorty interview.

13. Shorty interview.

14. John Morgan, interview by author, tape recording, Fort Wingate, NM, December 6, 2002.

15. Morgan interview.

16. Morgan interview.

17. Joann Thompson, interview by author, tape recording, Albuquerque, NM, October 13, 2002.

18. Thompson interview.

Chapter 5

1. U.S. Census Bureau, *American Indian and Alaska Native Population*.

2. Yazzie, *Navajo History*; Mike Mitchell, *Origins of the Diné* (Rough Rock, Ariz.: Navajo Studies and Curriculum Center, 2001).

3. New Mexico Department of Cultural Affairs, *The Story of Bosque Redondo* (Santa Fe: Department of Cultural Affairs and Museum of New Mexico, 2005).

4. Treaty Between the United States of America and the Navaho Tribe of Indians, July 25, 1868, 15 Stats., p. 667.

5. USA, Navaho Treaty.

6. New Mexico Department of Cultural Affairs, *Story of Bosque Redondo*.

7. Donald A. Grinde and Bruce E. Johansen, *Ecocide of Native America: Environmental Destruction of Indian Lands and Peoples* (Santa Fe, NM: Clear Light, 1995); Iverson, *Diné*, 219; Navajo Uranium Workers Oral History and Photography Project, Doug Brugge, coordinator, PIPC.

8. Iverson, *Diné*, 219; Grinde and Johansen, *Ecocide of Native America*, 208–9.

9. On the eastern part of the Navajo Nation, thousands of allotments are adjacent to the Navajo reservation boundaries. These allotments are fractionated tracts of land with approximately thousands of owners. The Cobell Settlement Agreement in 2011 allowed a consolidation fund to help purchase fractional interests for the Navajo Nation and numerous other Native Nations across the United States.

10. Luci Tapahonso, *A Radiant Curve: Poems and Stories* (Tucson: University of Arizona Press, 2008), 5.

11. Laura Tohe, *Tséyi' Deep in the Rock: Reflections on Canyon De Chelly* (Tucson: University of Arizona Press, 2005), 35.

12. Irvin Morris, *From the Glittering World: A Navajo Story* (Norman: University of Oklahoma Press, 1997), 33.

13. Quoted in Malcolm Benally, *Bitter Water: Diné Oral Histories of the Navajo-Hopi Land Dispute* (Tucson: University of Arizona Press, 2011), 23.

14. Quoted in M. Benally, *Bitter Water*, 30.

15. Quoted in M. Benally, *Bitter Water*, 52.

16. Quoted in M. Benally, *Bitter Water*, 59.

Conclusion

1. Yolynda Begay, "Historic and Demographic Changes that Impact the Future of the Diné and the Development of Community-Based Policy," in *Diné Perspectives: Revitalizing and Reclaiming Navajo Thought*, ed. Lloyd L. Lee (Tucson: University of Arizona Press, 2014), 108.

SELECTED BIBLIOGRAPHY

Alvord, Lori Arviso, and Elizabeth Cohen Van Pelt. *The Scalpel and the Silver Bear: The First Navajo Woman Surgeon Combines Western Medicine and Traditional Healing*. New York: Bantam Books, 1999.

Aronilth, Wilson, Jr. *Foundation of Culture*. Tsaile, Ariz.: Diné College, 1992.

Austin, Martha, and Regina Lynch, eds. *Saad Ahaah Sinil Dual Language: A Navajo-English Dictionary*. Rev. ed. Chinle, Ariz.: Rough Rock Press, 1990.

Austin, Raymond D. *Navajo Courts and Navajo Common Law: A Tradition of Tribal Self-Governance*. Minneapolis: University of Minnesota Press, 2009.

Bailey, Lynn Robinson. *Indian Slave Trade in the Southwest: A Study of Slave-Taking and the Traffic in Indian Captives*. Los Angeles, Calif.: Westernlore Press, 1966.

Begay, Yolynda. "Historic and Demographic Changes that Impact the Future of the Diné and the Development of Community-Based Policy." In *Diné Perspectives: Revitalizing and Reclaiming Navajo Thought*, edited by Lloyd L. Lee, 108. Tucson: University of Arizona Press, 2014.

Benally, Herbert John. "Navajo Philosophy of Learning and Pedagogy." *Journal of Navajo Education* 12, no. 1 (Fall 1994): 23–31.

Benally, Malcolm. *Bitter Water: Diné Oral Histories of the Navajo-Hopi Land Dispute*. Tucson: University of Arizona Press, 2011.

Brugge, David M. *Navajos in the Catholic Church Records of New Mexico, 1694–1875*. Tsaile, Ariz.: Navajo Community College Press, 1985.

Crawford, James. "Endangered Native American Languages: What Is to Be Done, and Why?" *Bilingual Research Journal* 19, no. 1 (Winter 1995): 17–38.

Farella, John. *The Main Stalk: A Synthesis of Navajo Philosophy.* Albuquerque: University of New Mexico Press, 1984.

Fishman, Joshua. *Reversing Language Shift.* Clevedon: Multilingual Matters, 1991.

Forbes, Jack D. "Blood Quantum: A Relic of Racism and Termination." The People's Voice, the Weyanoke Association, November 27, 2000. http://weyanoke.org/reading/jdf-BloodQuantum.html.

Frisbie, Charlotte. *Kinaaldá: A Study of the Navaho Girl's Puberty Ceremony.* Middletown, Conn.: Wesleyan University Press, 1967.

Goddard, Pliny Earle. "Navajo Texts." *Anthropological Papers of the American Museum of Natural History* 34 (1933): 1–179.

Goodluck, Charlotte. "Understanding Navajo Ethnic Identity: Weaving the Meaning through the Voices of Young Girls." PhD diss., University of Denver, 1998.

Grinde, Donald A., and Bruce E. Johansen. *Ecocide of Native America: Environmental Destruction of Indian Lands and Peoples.* Santa Fe, N.Mex.: Clear Light, 1995.

Haile, Berard. "Soul Concepts of the Navaho." *Annali Lateranensi* 7 (1943): 59–94.

Harvey, Karen D., and Lisa D. Harjo. *Indian Country: A History of Native People in America.* Golden, Colo.: North American Press, 1994.

Haskie, Miranda J. "Preserving a Culture: Practicing the Navajo Principles of Hózhó dóó Kʼé." Ph.D. diss., Fielding Graduate Institute, 2002.

Holm, Wayne, and Agnes Holm. "Navajo Language Education: Retrospect and Prospects." *Bilingual Research Journal* 19, no. 1 (1990): 141–67.

House, Deborah. *Language Shift Among the Navajos: Identity Politics and Cultural Continuity.* Tucson: University of Arizona Press, 2002.

Iverson, Peter. *Diné: A History of the Navajos.* Albuquerque: University of New Mexico, 2002.

Jacobsen, Kristina. *The Sound of Navajo Country: Music, Language, and Diné Belonging.* Chapel Hill: University of North Carolina Press, 2017.

Jim, Rex Lee. "A Moment in My Life." In *Here First: Autobiographical Essays by Native American Writers*, edited by Arnold Krupat and Brian Swann, 229–46. New York: Modern Library, 2000.

Kluckhohn, Clyde. "The Philosophy of Navaho Indians." In *Readings in Anthropology*, vol. 2, edited by Morton H. Fried, 424–49. New York: Crowell, 1959.

Kristofic, Jim. *The Hero Twins: A Navajo-English Story of the Monster Slayer*. English and Navajo ed. Albuquerque: University of New Mexico Press, 2015.

Lee, Lloyd L. "21st Century Diné Cultural Identity: Defining and Practicing Sa'ah Naaghai Bik'eh Hozhoon." PhD diss., University of New Mexico, 2004.

Lee, Lloyd L. *Diné Masculinities: Conceptualizations and Reflections*. North Charleston, S.C.: CreateSpace, 2013.

Lee, Lloyd L., ed. *Diné Perspectives: Revitalizing and Reclaiming Navajo Thought*. Tucson: University of Arizona Press, 2014.

Lee, Lloyd L., ed. *Navajo Sovereignty: Understandings and Visions of the Diné People*. Tucson: University of Arizona Press, 2017.

Lee, Tiffany S. "If They Want Navajo to Be Learned, Then They Should Require It in All Schools: Navajo Teenagers' Experiences, Choices, and Demands Regarding Navajo Language," *Wicazo Sa Review* 22, no. 1 (Spring 2007): 7–33.

McAllester, David P. *Hogans: Navajo Houses and House Songs*. Middletown, CT: Wesleyan University Press, 1987.

McCarty, Teresa L., Mary Romero-Little, and Ofelia Zepeda. "Native American Youth Discourses on Language Shift and Retention: Ideological Cross-Currents and Their Implications for Language Planning." *International Journal of Bilingual Education and Bilingualism* 9, no. 5 (2006): 659–77.

McNitt, Frank. *Navajo Wars: Military Campaigns, Slave Raids, and Reprisals*. Albuquerque: University of New Mexico Press, 1972.

McPherson, Robert S. *Dinéjí Na'nitin: Navajo Traditional Teachings and History*. Boulder: University Press of Colorado, 2012.

Mitchell, Mike. *Origins of the Diné*. Rough Rock, Ariz.: Navajo Studies and Curriculum Center, 2001.

Morris, Irvin. *From the Glittering World: A Navajo Story*. Norman: University of Oklahoma Press, 1997.

New Mexico Department of Cultural Affairs. *The Story of Bosque Redondo*. Santa Fe: Department of Cultural Affairs and Museum of New Mexico, 2005.

Parsons-Yazzie, Evangeline. "Navajo-Speaking Parents' Perceptions of Reasons for Navajo Language Attrition." *Journal of Navajo Education* 13, no. 1 (1995): 29–38.

Parsons-Yazzie, Evangeline. "Perceptions of Selected Navajo Elders Regarding Navajo Language Attrition." *Journal of Navajo Education* 12, no. 2 (1996): 51–57.

Pavlik, Steve. "Navajo Christianity: Historical Origins and Modern Trends." *Wicazo Sa Review* 12, no. 2 (Fall 1997): 43–58.

Platero, Paul. *Navajo Head Start Language Study*. Window Rock, Navajo Nation: Division of Diné Education, 1992.

Roessel, Ruth. *Women in Navajo Society*. Rough Rock, Ariz.: Navajo Resource Center, 1981.

Roessel, Ruth, and Broderick H. Johnson. *Navajo Livestock Reduction: A National Disgrace*. Chinle, Ariz.: Navajo Community College Press, 1974.

Schulz, Amy J. "Navajo Women and the Politics of Identity." *Social Problems* 45 (1998): 3, 336–55.

Slate, Clay. "On Reversing Navajo Language Shift." *Journal of Navajo Education* 10, no. 3 (1993): 30–35.

Spruhan, Paul. "The Origins, Current Status, and Future Prospects of Blood Quantum as the Definition of Membership in the Navajo Nation." *Tribal Law Journal* 8, no. 1 (2007): 1–17.

Tapahonso, Luci. *A Radiant Curve: Poems and Stories*. Tucson: University of Arizona Press, 2008.

Tohe, Laura. *Tséyi' Deep in the Rock: Reflections on Canyon De Chelly*. Tucson: University of Arizona Press, 2005.

U.S. Bureau of the Census. *The American Indian and Alaska Native Population: 2010*. Washington, D.C.: Department of Commerce, Economics and Statistics Administration, Bureau of the Census.

Wheelwright, Mary C. *Navajo Creation Myth*. Santa Fe, N.Mex.: Museum of Navajo Ceremonial Art, 1942.

Witherspoon, Gary. *Language and Art in the Navajo Universe*. Ann Arbor: University of Michigan Press, 1977.

Wyman, Leland. *Blessingway*. Tucson: University of Arizona Press, 1970.

Yazzie, Ethelou, ed. *Navajo History*. Vol. 1. Rough Rock, Ariz.: Navajo Curriculum Center, 1971.

INDEX

ABOUT THE AUTHOR

Lloyd L. Lee is a citizen of the Navajo Nation. He is an associate professor of Native American studies at the University of New Mexico. His research focuses on identity, masculinities, leadership, philosophies, and Native nation building.